PET
Testbuilder

Lucrecia Luque-Mortimer

MACMILLAN

Macmillan Education
Between Towns Road, Oxford OX4 3PP
A division of Macmillan Publishers Limited
Companies and representatives throughout the world

ISBN 10: 1-4050-6298-3 (with key edition)
ISBN 13: 978-1-4050-6298-5
ISBN 10: 1-4050-6299-1 (without key edition)
ISBN 13: 978-1-4050-6299-2
ISBN 10: 1-4050-6301-7 (with key pack)
ISBN 13: 978-1-4050-6301-2

Text © Lucrecia Luque-Mortimer 2005
Design and illustration © Macmillan Publishers Limited 2005

First published 2005

Original design by Xen Media Ltd
Page layout by eMC Design, www.emcdesign.org.uk
Illustrated by Stephen Dew, Ivan Gillet, Janos Jantner and
Tony Wilkins
Cover design by Xen Media Ltd

The author and publishers would like to thank Nelson Aurich and his
students at the Academia Argentina de Cultura Inglesa in Alta
Gracia, Cordoba and the staff and students at Reading College for
their contributions.

The author and publishers would like to thank Sarah Dymond for her
invaluable comments.

The author and publishers would like to thank the following for
permission to reprint the following copyright material:
Extract from 'Jura – more deer than people' by Alex Dunnachie,
taken from *Holiday West Highland* 2003; Extract from 'West Wales'
by Patricia Link, first published in *Woman's Weekly Travel* magazine;
Extract from 'An unusual inventor' by Margaret Knight, taken from
www.voicesofinnovation.org, 15.04.03, reprinted by permission of
the publisher; Extract from article by J E Bedi from
www.hrw.com/science/si-science/chemistry/careers/innovativelives/
womeninventors.html; Extract from 'Travelling first class' by Jeremy
Hart copyright © Jeremy Hart 2004, first published in *Sunday Times
Travel* Magazine April/May 2004, reprinted by permission of News
International Limited; Extract from 'From schoolboy to clown' by
Richard Barber, first published in *Sainsbury's* Magazine October
2002, reprinted by permission of the publisher.

The authors and publishers would like to thank the following for
permission to reproduce photographs their photographic material:
Alamy / Janie Woedel pp122, 126; Corbis / Mike Southern p125;
Getty p120; Rex / Blair Beitz p124, Rex / Patrick Frillet p123, Rex /
Geoff Wolkinson p127; Stone p121.

Whilst every effort has been made to locate the owners of copyright
material in this book, there may have been some cases when the
publishers have been unable to contact the owners. We should be
grateful to hear from anyone who recognises copyright material and
who is unacknowledged. We shall be pleased to make the necessary
ammendments in future editions of the book.

Printed and bound in Spain by Edelvives

2009 2008 2007 2006
10 9 8 7 6 5 4 3 2

CONTENTS

Introduction 4

INTRODUCTION

The PET Testbuilder

The Preliminary English Test (PET) Testbuilder provides students with the information, advice and practice they need to pass PET. It offers teachers and students an encouraging and accessible way to prepare for the exam and may be used as part of an English language course or as a self-access programme for students preparing for the exam on their own. There are four complete practice tests that reflect the content and level of the actual examination. All the tests are of a similar standard and include the themes, topics and vocabulary specified in the PET syllabus. They are accompanied by an expanded answer key, an Exam Information and Advice and a Further Practice and Guidance section for each part of the test.

Expanded Key

The main purpose of the expanded key is to promote confidence and understanding of the demands of the exam. It gives students and teachers information about why a particular answer is correct and, when appropriate, there are explanations as to why other options or possible answers are incorrect.

Exam Information and Advice

Each part of the test has an Exam Information and Advice section. The aim of this section is to show students what they are expected to do and the best way of tackling the particular items in each part of the test.

Further Practice and Guidance

Each part of the test has a graduated exercise to enable students to improve their test technique as well as their language skills.

The Preliminary English Test

The PET covers the four language skills of reading, writing, listening and speaking. At Preliminary level, the reading and writing skills are combined in one question paper.

Reading and Writing (1 hour 30 minutes)

Reading

The reading test is in five parts. There is one mark for each question.

Part One

This consists of five short texts, for example, signs, messages, notes, emails. Each text is followed by a multiple-choice question. This part tests the ability to read real-world notices and other short texts for the main message. See page 8 for more information and advice.

Part Two

This consists of five short descriptions of people and eight short texts. The task is to match each person with the correct text. This part tests the ability to read multiple texts for specific information and detailed comprehension. See page 38 for more information and advice.

Part Three

This consists of a factual text of 400–450 words, taken from a travel brochure, an advertisement, a magazine, etc. The text is followed by ten statements, and the task is to decide which statements are True and which are False. This part tests the ability to find specific information in a text and disregard redundant material. See page 68 for more information and advice.

Part Four

This consists of a text of 220–280 words, taken from a newspaper, a magazine, a review, etc. The text is followed by five multiple-choice questions, each with four options. This part tests the ability to understand attitude, opinion and the purpose of the writer. See page 98 for more information and advice.

Part Five

This consists of a factual or narrative text of 125–150 words, followed by ten multiple-choice questions, each with four options. This part tests the ability to understand vocabulary and grammar in a short text. See page 100 for more information and advice.

Writing

The writing test is in three parts.

Part One (Questions 1–5)

In this task there are five complete sentences on the same topic. Below each one, there is an incomplete sentence. The task is to complete it so that it means the same as the complete sentence. This part tests control of and understanding of grammatical structures. There is one mark for each sentence. See page 18 for more information and advice.

Part Two (Question 6)

The task is to produce a short communicative message of between 35 and 45 words in length. There is a clear situation which tells the student who to write to and why, followed by three content points. This part tests the ability to communicate specific information. There are five marks for this part. See page 47 for more information and advice.

Part Three

The task is to produce a longer piece of writing, of about 100 words. There is a choice of an informal letter or a story. For the story, either the title or the first sentence is provided. This part tests the ability to use and control a range of PET level language. There are 15 marks for this part. See pages 76 and 105 for more information and advice.

Listening (approximately 30 minutes)

The listening test consists of a series of recorded texts and a written question paper. In the exam, all the instructions are on the recording and on the question paper. The test is in four parts. Each part is played twice. In the exam itself, there is an extra six minutes to transfer the answers on to a special computer-marked answer sheet. There is one mark for each question (a total of 25 questions).

Part One

This consists of seven short conversations or monologues (when one person is speaking). Each recording is played twice. There are seven multiple-choice questions with three visual choices or options. The task is to listen and choose the correct option. This part tests the ability to understand factual information. See page 24 for more information and advice.

Part Two

This consists of a longer text which can be either a monologue or an interview with questions from a radio presenter. The recording is played twice. There are six multiple-choice questions with three choices or options. This part tests the ability to understand the general meaning of the text and find specific information. See page 53 for more information and advice.

Part Three

This consists of a longer text which is an informational monologue. The recording is played twice. On the page, there are notes with six blank spaces or gaps. The task is to fill in the gaps with words from the text. This part tests the ability to understand and write down specific information from the text. See page 82 for more information and advice.

Part Four

This consists of a longer text which is an informal conversation between two people, generally one male and one female. They discuss their attitudes and opinions on a given topic. The recording is played twice. On the page, there are six statements which report the speakers' attitudes and opinions. The task is to decide whether each statement is True or False. This part tests the ability to understand the general meaning of the conversation and the speakers' attitudes, opinions, agreement and disagreement. See page 113 for more information and advice.

Speaking (10–12 minutes per pair of candidates)

The speaking test is taken in pairs and, occasionally, with three candidates. There are two examiners. One of them (the interlocutor) speaks to the candidates and leads them through the tasks. The other examiner just listens. The test is in four parts.

Part One (2–3 minutes)

In this part the interlocutor talks to each of the candidates in turn and asks general questions about where they live and work, what they are studying or what they do in their spare time. This part tests the ability to give personal information about the present, the past or the future. See page 29 for more information and advice.

Part Two (2–3 minutes)

In this part, the two candidates discuss a simulated situation, using a visual aid to help them. The interlocutor just listens while the candidates talk to each other. This part tests the ability to make and respond to suggestions, discuss alternatives, give opinions, etc. See page 58 for more information and advice.

Part Three (3 minutes)

In this part, each candidate in turn describes a photograph, giving a description of what he/she can see. The two photographs have a common theme. This part tests the ability to use vocabulary and structures to give a simple description which lasts between 45 seconds and 1 minute. See page 87 for more information and advice.

Part Four (3 minutes)

This part is a conversation between the candidates. The theme of the photographs they have just described is the starting point for the discussion. This part tests the ability to talk about – and give reasons for – personal opinions, likes and dislikes. See page 118 for more information and advice.

TEST ONE

PAPER 1: READING 1 hour

PART ONE

Questions 1–5

- Look at the text in each question.
- What does it say?
- Mark the correct letter (**A**, **B** or **C**).

- *In the exam you will mark your answers on a separate answer sheet (see page 33).*

Example:

0

A There will be delays on night trains tomorrow.

B There will be two night trains every hour tomorrow.

C There will be more night trains from platform 6 tomorrow.

Answer: | **0** | A ~~B~~ C |

1

MESSAGE

Mary
A message from the furniture shop:
they will deliver your chair tomorrow
at 2 p.m. Be home from work
by then – I'll be out.
            Sylvia

A Sylvia will try to be home by 2 p.m.

B Mary has to be home by 2 p.m.

C Mary must phone the shop by 2 p.m.

2

Tuesday 15
The museum is closed
for repairs until Sunday
– normal opening hours
from Monday.

A The museum can't be visited until Monday because of repair work.

B The museum will close from next Monday because of repair work.

C The museum is closed until Monday and will re-open on Tuesday.

3

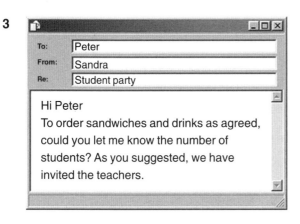

A   Sandra would like Peter to invite some of their teachers to the party.

B   Sandra and Peter are responsible for getting food for the party.

C   Peter needs to give Sandra some details about the party.

4

A   After you use books, put them back on the shelves.

B   Leave books on the table when you finish using them.

C   If you find books on tables, take them to the librarian.

5

A   Tell children that they should not touch this.

B   Use this product only with older children.

C   Put this product where children cannot touch it.

Before doing this part of the test, read the Exam Information and Advice on the next page.

EXAM INFORMATION AND ADVICE

Part One tests your understanding of various kinds of short texts. These may be:

- public notices and signs
- instructions/information on packages or bottles
- notes, emails, cards or postcards.

With each text there is a multiple-choice question with three options: A, B and C.

1   First read the text carefully to understand the general meaning of the text.

Example 0: This is a passenger information notice at a railway station. It gives information about train departure times.

2   Look at the background of the text (the visual information). It may help you to understand the situation and the purpose of the text.

Example 0: The artwork shows a computer screen, probably in an area of the station where passengers can see it clearly.

3   Read all three options carefully.

*Example 0: **A** mentions delays to train services tomorrow night. **B** mentions two train services per hour tomorrow night. **C** mentions more night trains tomorrow.*

4   Compare each option with the text and then choose one of them.

*Option **A**: the text does not say anything about trains being late, so this is the wrong option. Option **B**: the text says there will be one train at 20 minutes past the hour and another one at 40 minutes past the hour, which means there will be two trains every hour. This must be the correct option. Option **C**: the text does not say that there are going to be more trains than usual, so this is the wrong option.*

5   Look again at the incorrect options and underline the words that show that they are wrong.

***A**: There will be <u>delays</u> on night trains tomorrow.*
***C**: There will be <u>more night trains</u> from platform 6 tomorrow.*

6   Re-read the text and the option you chose to make sure it is the correct answer.

***Text**: Tomorrow - Platform 6   Night trains leave at <u>20 and 40 minutes past the hour</u>*
***B**: There will be <u>two night trains every hour tomorrow</u>.*

A DETAILED STUDY

The questions below will help you to make sure that you have chosen the correct options.

1   Think of the location of each text. Match each text (1–5) in Part One to the place (a–f)
     where you would find them. One location does not match any of the texts!

   a)   on the front door of a building

   b)   in a library

   c)   in a classroom

   d)   on a table by the telephone

   e)   on a bottle

   f)   on a computer screen

2   Think of the purpose of each text. Match each text (1–5) in Part One to an action (a–f)
     that may follow. One action does not follow any of the texts!

   a)   Leave books on a library table.

   b)   Go home and come back next week.

   c)   Ask your boss if you can leave work early tomorrow.

   d)   Find some information and send it.

   e)   Go in and buy something.

   f)   Find a safe place to store something.

Now check your answers to Part One again and decide if you want to change anything.

PART TWO

Questions 6–10

- The people below all want to find a job connected with travelling.
- On the opposite page there are descriptions of eight jobs.
- Decide which job would be the most suitable for the following people.
- For questions **6–10**, mark the correct letter (**A–H**).

- *In the exam you will mark your answers on a separate answer sheet (see page 33).*

6

Carl used to work as a reporter. He wants a job which involves travelling and also writing about his experiences. He does not mind spending long periods abroad and he could start tomorrow.

7

Debbie has a degree in Zoology and wants a job where she can use that knowledge and also travel. She works well with other people and speaks German. She is not keen on sports.

8

Pedro is looking for an exciting summer job where he can learn new skills. He was trained as a deep-sea diver and has taken groups of children and adults on diving trips.

9

Jackie wants a job that will allow her to spend several months abroad. She can hold a simple conversation in Spanish and French. She used to take London tourists sightseeing in her own car.

10

Clara is a tourist guide, but now she has a small child and she wants a job which does not require her to travel abroad. She speaks Spanish and she is willing to work at weekends.

The London Job Centre

DO YOU WANT AN EXCITING JOB? CHECK THESE GREAT OPPORTUNITIES ...

A **Walk the World** needs an experienced traveller to organize walking tours for families, schools and college groups. The job is for two years and involves short trips abroad to find walking routes suitable for different levels of fitness. A knowledge of languages would be an advantage.

E **World Wildlife,** the designer of group wildlife holidays around the world, requires a tour guide. You must have knowledge of animals, be a real team player and be able to speak at least one foreign language. No previous experience as a tour guide needed. The job starts in three weeks' time.

B **Gordon Trips** needs an employee to help organize European tours. Foreign travel is not in the job description, but you will have contact by email and telephone with clients, so you must speak French or Spanish or German. We work on Saturdays in the summer months.

F **Global Tourism** is looking for two people with an excellent command of Spanish and English to accompany groups of English-speaking tourists on whale-watching trips to South America. You must be fit and a good swimmer. These are one-year jobs starting next summer.

C **Super Travel** is developing its Asian adventure team and is looking for a team leader to cover the summer months. We will give you training in climbing and trekking, but you must have excellent swimming skills. Some experience of working with different age groups is essential.

G *Worldwide* **Magazine** is looking for a travel writer to cover Central and West Africa, starting immediately. The job is mostly based in our central office, but you must be willing to spend at least two weeks a month travelling. Previous experience of journalism is essential.

D **Life of Adventure Publishers** urgently needs a reporter with experience of deep-sea photography to join its team in Jamaica. The job is for the summer and we offer all the equipment and comfortable accommodation for a family group if requested. Excellent salary and free weekends.

H **Kanco Expeditions** is looking for leaders for its Latin American tours. You must have a driving licence and a basic knowledge of Spanish. The job will require you to spend up to six months per year in Central and South America. Extensive travel experience is not essential.

Before doing this part of the test, read the Exam Information and Advice on page 38.

PART THREE
Questions 11–20

- Look at the sentences below about the island of Jura in Scotland.
- Read the text on the opposite page to decide if each sentence is correct or incorrect.
- If it is correct, mark **A**.
- If it is not correct, mark **B**.

- *In the exam you will mark your answers on a separate sheet (see page 33).*

---

11   The people who live in Jura would like to have more excitement in their lives.

12   Walkers are advised to start the climbing of a hill in the morning.

13   Visitors can expect to see wildlife as soon as they arrive in Jura.

14   Visitors should avoid the use of a flash when photographing wild animals.

15   At Ardfin gardens, a tour guide gives visitors information about walks.

16   The path for the garden walks divides in two before visitors cross the stream.

17   The walled garden has a display of plants from different parts of the world.

18   The Jura Hotel prices are higher than in other similar hotels in Scotland.

19   Visitors are unable to buy camping equipment at Jura Stores.

20   Visitors can order items from Jura Stores before they arrive on the island.

Before doing this part of the test, read the Exam Information and Advice on page 68.

THE ISLAND OF JURA

The Island of Jura is one of Scotland's best kept secrets – a beautiful but little known island with a population of some 200 people. The quiet life of Jura would be hard to find anywhere else, and the inhabitants of Jura are proud of that. However, if you want an active holiday, there are many things for you to see and do.

Climb the hills

If you enjoy walking and hill climbing, for example, then the hills of Jura, which rise to more than 800 metres, should be on your list. As these walks take about seven hours, strong walking boots are recommended and an early start is essential for a safe return before dark.

Enjoy the wildlife

Beautiful birds, seals, golden eagles … From the moment you get off the Jura ferry at Feolin, the chances are that you will see deer happily feeding on sea plants along the shoreline. In fact, you would do well to have a camera with a flash within easy reach, as there will be many opportunities to get those special once-in-a-lifetime photographs.

Visit the Ardfin Gardens

They are open all year round. Entry is through the main gate, where you will find an information board and a box with maps and short guides to the two garden walks you can do. The beginning of both walks will take you over a small stream. It is here that you turn left to do the longer of the two walks along the cliff tops. The views are spectacular and on a clear day you will be able to see as far as Northern Ireland. Back at sea level, do not forget to visit the walled garden. Here you will see native plants mixed with plants from far-away countries.

Where to stay and shop

The island has only one large hotel. The Jura Hotel offers visitors a warm and friendly atmosphere and an excellent menu, and their prices are what you would expect to pay in other parts of Scotland. For those wishing to camp on Jura, the hotel field is excellent, with shower facilities at the back of the hotel. Just opposite the hotel is 'Jura Stores'. From the outside it looks like any other small village shop. However, once inside you will be surprised at the selection of goods on offer – from delicious cakes to waterproofs and sleeping bags. Steve (the owner) has built his own website, so you can email him and have the goods you need delivered to your accommodation for your arrival.

So why not spend a few days on Jura? You will come away feeling refreshed, invigorated and planning your next visit …

PART FOUR

Questions 21–25

- Read the text and questions below.
- For each question, mark the correct letter (**A**, **B**, **C** or **D**).

- *In the exam you will mark your answers on a separate answer sheet (see page 33).*

Jim Benson, pianist and songwriter

People often ask me who I have to thank for my success as a pianist and songwriter. They expect to hear that I was born into a musical family and had an excellent piano teacher. However, the truth is different. When I was little, nobody played an instrument at home. I learnt to play the piano and sing because there was a piano in my house and I just wanted to make music.

My parents allowed me to sit at the piano and sing for as long as I wanted. If they were afraid that I would break the old piano, they never mentioned it. They didn't suggest that I should take lessons, either. The songs just came to me when I had my hands on the piano. I suppose I had musical talent and that is all you need.

I started writing proper songs when I was a teenager. The music was mine, but the words were from other song writers. It seemed so easy. When you start to compose, you do that, you copy other people's best songs. Then you start changing the melodies and the words and you develop your own style. That only happened later, when I had grown beyond my teenage years.

For a time, I thought music would be just a hobby. My parents had developed a strong belief that I would be able to make a living as a musician, but I had my doubts, so after school I took a job in radio advertising. Then one day one of my songs won a prize and that changed everything. I realized my happiness was in music. I have been a musician ever since that day.

---

21   What is Jim Benson's main purpose in writing the text?

    A   to suggest how children can be taught music

    B   to describe his life as a successful musician

    C   to explain how he became a musician

    D   to complain about his lack of musical training

22   When Jim Benson started making music on the piano, his parents

    A   seemed happy to let him play it.

    B   said the piano might get damaged.

    C   saw the need for a piano teacher.

    D   wanted him to play his own songs.

23   What does Jim Benson say about the songs he wrote as a teenager?

    A   They were not well-written.

    B   They took a long time to write.

    C   They were not very original.

    D   They showed his personal style.

24   Jim Benson took a job in advertising because

    A   his parents suggested it was a good career for him.

    B   he thought he might not earn enough as a musician.

    C   he had learnt about advertising jobs at school.

    D   it offered him the opportunity to change his life.

25   Which advice would Jim Benson give talented young people?

A

You need somebody in your family to guide you when you start.

B
It's OK to copy other people's songs when you are learning.

C

It is not a good idea to write songs when you are very young.

D
If you want to be successful, you must have good music teachers.

Before doing this part of the test, read the Exam Information and Advice on page 98.

PART FIVE
Questions 26–35

- Read the text below and choose the correct word for each space.
- For each question, mark the correct letter (**A, B, C** or **D**).

- *In the exam you will mark your answers on a separate answer sheet (see page 33).*

Example:

0 **A** watching   **B** looking   **C** appearing   **D** hearing

Answer: | 0 | A | B | C | D |

DOLPHINS IN WALES

I fell in love with the Welsh landscape after **(0)** .... a television programme about dolphins off the west coast. I decided to **(26)** .... a holiday there. The programme **(27)** .... the best place to see them was Cardigan Bay and the best **(28)** .... was late afternoon.

The first evening I expected a long wait, **(29)** .... I sat on a bench with some fish and chips. **(30)** .... other people were there and after a few minutes we heard a child's voice cry out, 'There!' The dolphins had arrived and they were playing and **(31)** .... fun. It was wonderful to see them as they **(32)** .... always be – free.

I also **(33)** .... out that this area has beautiful beaches and fantastic castles to explore. It was the first time I had **(34)** .... in Wales and I knew it would not be the last. I have returned **(35)** .... the same place several times.

26	**A**	tour	**B**	pass	**C**	spend	**D**	stay
27	**A**	told	**B**	said	**C**	talked	**D**	spoke
28	**A**	period	**B**	hour	**C**	part	**D**	time
29	**A**	so	**B**	since	**C**	but	**D**	because
30	**A**	Lots	**B**	All	**C**	Many	**D**	Much
31	**A**	feeling	**B**	getting	**C**	enjoying	**D**	having
32	**A**	ought	**B**	should	**C**	have	**D**	could
33	**A**	looked	**B**	realized	**C**	found	**D**	learnt
34	**A**	been	**B**	visited	**C**	come	**D**	gone
35	**A**	to	**B**	for	**C**	at	**D**	on

Before doing this part of the test, read the Exam Information and Advice on page 100.

PAPER 1: WRITING 30 minutes

PART ONE
Questions 1–5

- Here are some sentences about reading.
- For each question, complete the second sentence so that it means the same as the first.
- **Use no more than three words.**
- Write only the missing words.

- *In the exam you will write your answers on a separate answer sheet (see page 89).*

Example:

0   I spend an hour reading the newspaper every day.

  It takes me an hour .... **the newspaper every day.**

Answer: | 0 | *to read* |

---

1   I haven't read a good novel for a long time.

  It's a long time .... **I read a good novel.**

2   Why don't you borrow a book from the library?

  If I were you, I .... **a book from the library.**

3   I think that history books are more interesting than novels.

  I think that novels are not .... **history books.**

4   There aren't many history books in my local library.

  My local library has only got a .... **history books.**

5   My brother is too young to read computer books.

  My brother isn't .... **to read computer books.**

Before doing this part of the test, read the Exam Information and Advice on the next page.

EXAM INFORMATION AND ADVICE

Part One is a sentence transformation task, which tests your understanding of grammatical structures. You get five complete sentences, with an incomplete sentence below each one. You have to complete these five sentences using one, two or three words. The sentence you complete must mean the same as the first sentence.

Always read the example because it shows you exactly what you have to do.

The five sentences are always on the same topic or theme. Read them all to understand the topic. After you write the word(s), read each full sentence to yourself and then compare it carefully with the first sentence. Is the meaning the same?

Remember: you must spell the word(s) correctly in this part and you must not write more than three words (contractions, i.e. *isn't, don't*, count as two words). Finally, practise writing only the missing words on the answer sheet (page 89).

For this part of the test, revise your grammar, i.e. tenses, modal verbs, passive and active forms, direct and indirect speech.

A DETAILED STUDY

Look again at questions 1–5 on page 17 and then decide which of the three answers below is the right way to complete each sentence.

1   **a)**   It's a long time that I read a good novel.

    b)   It's a long time since I read a good novel.

    c)   It's a long time before I read a good novel.

2   **a)**   If I were you, I would to borrow a book from the library.

    b)   If I were you, I would borow a book from the library.

    c)   If I were you, I would borrow a book from the library.

3   **a)**   I think that novels are not as interesting as history books.

    b)   I think that novels are not less interesting than history books.

    c)   I think that novels are not very interesting as history books

4   **a)**   My local library has only got a number of history books.

    b)   My local library has only got a few history books.

    c)   My local library has only got a few of history books.

5   **a)**   My brother isn't as old as to read computer books.

    b)   My brother isn't too old to read computer books.

    c)   My brother isn't old enough to read computer books.

Now check your answers to Part One and see if you want to change anything.

PART TWO

Question 6

You want to go to the cinema with your English friend, Jack.

Write an email to Jack. In your email, you should

- say what film you want to see

- invite Jack to see it

- suggest a time and place to meet.

Write **35–45 words**.

- *In the exam you will write your answer on a separate answer sheet (see page 89).*

Before you write your answer, read the Exam Information and Advice on page 47.

PART THREE

Questions 7–8

Write an answer to **one** of the questions (**7** or **8**).

Write about **100 words**.

Question 7

- This is part of a letter you receive from your English friend John.

> I'm reading a great novel. Do you read books or magazines? Tell me about something you've read recently.

- Now write a letter, answering your friend's questions.
- Write your **letter** in about 100 words.

- *In the exam you will write your answer on a separate answer sheet (see page 89).*

Question 8

- Your English teacher has asked you to write a story.
- Your story must begin with this sentence:

> *Tom was watching TV at home when he heard a noise upstairs.*

- Write your **story** in about 100 words.

- *In the exam you will write your answer on a separate answer sheet (see page 89).*

Before you write your letter, read the Exam Information and Advice for Question 7 on page 76.

Before you write your story, read the Exam Information and Advice for Question 8 on page 105.

PAPER 2: LISTENING

PART ONE
Questions 1–7

- There are seven questions in this part.
- For each question there are three pictures and a short recording.
- Choose the correct picture and put a tick (✔) in the box below it.

- *In the exam you will write your answers on the question paper and then you will have six minutes to copy them on to the answer sheet (see page 119).*

Example: Which musical instrument will the man buy?

A   B ☐   C ☐

---

1   What will the woman wear at the party?

A ☐   B ☐   C ☐

2   Where will Charles meet Bob?

A ☐   B ☐   C ☐

3   When is the lecture?

A ☐   B ☐   C ☐

4   What did the man borrow from the library?

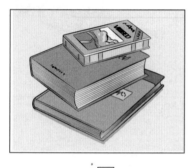      

A ☐   B ☐   C ☐

5   How did the man learn about the cycling race?

A ☐   B ☐   C ☐

6   What did they watch on TV yesterday?

A ☐   B ☐   C ☐

7   Which activity can people under 14 do alone?

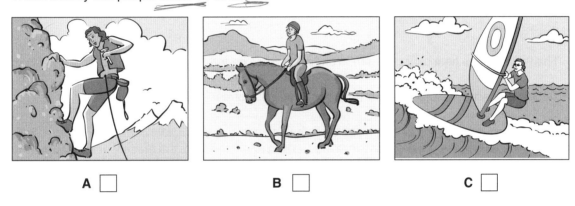

A ☐   B ☐   C ☐

Before doing this part of the test, read the Exam Information and Advice on the next page.

EXAM INFORMATION AND ADVICE

In Part One, you listen to seven short dialogues or monologues. For each one, there is a question and three visual images (pictures). You have to choose the picture that answers the question and tick the box below it. You will hear each piece twice. The dialogues/monologues may be:

- conversations at home or between friends
- conversations at college or at work
- conversations in shops
- answerphone messages
- radio announcements
- part of a talk.

1   Read the question very carefully. It tells you what information you have to listen for.

2   Look at the three pictures. The speaker(s) will mention all of them, but only one will be the correct answer.

3   The first time you hear a piece, listen to understand the general meaning and choose the best option.

4   During the second listening, check that your answer is correct.

Remember: the answer to the question can be at the beginning, in the middle or at the end. You need to understand the tenses the speakers use: Are they talking about the past, the present or the future?

A DETAILED STUDY

1   Before listening, read through the list below and decide for each question **1–7** (on pages 21–23), what you are listening for:

a)   the way a message was received

b)   a date

c)   a sport

d)   items of clothing

e)   the name of a programme

f)   a place

g)   object(s)

2   Now listen to Part One once and say if each text is:

a)   a conversation between friends/family

b)   an announcement (a monologue)

c)   an answerphone message

Check your answers. Then listen again and answer questions 1–7 in Part One.

PART TWO

Questions 8–13

- You will hear an interview with a woman who works in a museum.
- For each question, put a tick (✔) in the correct box.

- *In the exam you will write your answers on the question paper and then you will have six minutes to copy them on to the answer sheet (see page 119).*

---

8 When she was at school, Clara wanted to become

    A an actress. ☐

    B a teacher. ☐

    C a lawyer. ☐

9 Why did Clara not apply for the museum job sooner?

    A Her mother advised her to wait. ☐

    B It seemed a very difficult job. ☐

    C She thought it might be boring. ☐

10 What surprised Clara on her first day at work?

    A She had to carry some items. ☐

    B She was asked to give a speech. ☐

    C She had to meet lots of people. ☐

11 Clara was told to improve her knowledge of

    A computers. ☐

    B languages. ☐

    C mathematics. ☐

12 What part of her job does Clara enjoy most?

    A planning large exhibitions ☐

    B writing descriptions of objects ☐

    C talking to visitors about the displays ☐

13 What is Clara going to do next year?

    A finish her studies ☐

    B do some work abroad ☐

    C plan a new exhibition ☐

Before doing this part of the test, read the Exam Information and Advice on page 53.

PART THREE

Questions 14–19

- You will hear a man talking to a group of people about a new sports centre.
- For each question, fill in the missing information in the numbered space.

- *In the exam you will write your answers on the question paper and then you will have six minutes to copy them on to the answer sheet (see page 119).*

NEW SPORTS CENTRE

Facilities:

- swimming pool

- **(14)** ……………………………

- squash courts

- tennis court (opening on: **(15)** ………………………………)

Prices:

- Monthly: £35

- **(16)** £ ………………………… a year

  (special discounts for children)

- not included in price: equipment and swimming **(17)** ……………………………………

How to become a member:

Fill in a membership form – remember to write your **(18)** ………… and your weight.

For more information phone Mrs **(19)** ……………………………… on 467 9900.

Before doing this part of the test, read the Exam Information and Advice on page 82.

PART FOUR

Questions 20–25

- Look at the six sentences for this part.
- You will hear a conversation between a man, Jack, and a woman, Lara, about acting in a play.
- Decide if each sentence is correct or incorrect.
- If it is correct, put a tick (✔) in the box under **A** for **YES**. If it is not correct, put a tick (✔) in the box under **B** for **NO**.

- *In the exam you will write your answers on the question paper and then you will have six minutes to copy them on to the answer sheet (see page 119).*

		A YES	B NO
20	Lara is confident that the play will be a success.	☐	☐
21	Jack enjoyed acting when he was a child.	☐	☐
22	Lara thinks that Jack's voice was better when he was younger.	☐	☐
23	Jack expected Lara to have a successful career in acting.	☐	☐
24	Jack agrees to spend time reading the play.	☐	☐
25	Lara will try to change the date for the play.	☐	☐

Before doing this part of the test, read the Exam Information and Advice on page 113.

SPEAKING

PART ONE (2–3 minutes)

In Part One the examiner (interlocutor) will ask each of you some personal questions – your name, where you live, about your work or studies, about your free time activities, etc. The questions can be about the past, the present or the future.

Preliminary English Test
Speaking Test

Part 1 (2–3 minutes)

Phase 1
Interlocutor

**A/B   Good morning / afternoon / evening.
Can I have your mark sheets, please?**

**A/B   I'm .... and this is ....
He/she is just going to listen to us.**

**A   Now, what's your name?
Thank you.**

**B   And, what's your name?
Thank you.**

Back-up prompts

B What's your surname? **How do you spell it?** **Thank you.** **A And, what's your surname?** **How do you spell it?** **Thank you.**	**How do you write your family/second name?**
(Ask the following questions. Ask A first) **Where do you live / come from?** **Do you work or are you a student in ...?** **What do you do / study?** **Thank you.** **(Repeat for B)**	**Do you live in ...?** **Have you got a job?** **What job do you do? / What subject(s) do you study?**

Phase 2
(Select one or more questions from the list to ask each candidate. Ask Candidate B first.)

Do you enjoy studying English? Why (not)?

Do you think that English will be useful for you in the future?

What did you do yesterday evening / last weekend?

What do you enjoy doing in your free time?

Thank you.

(Introduction to Part 2)
In the next part, you are going to talk to each other.

Before doing this part of the test, read the Exam Information and Advice on the next page.

EXAM INFORMATION AND ADVICE

In Part One, the examiner will first introduce him/herself and the co-examiner and then he/she will ask you and your partner (the other candidate) the SAME questions about your personal details (your name, how you spell your surname, where you live, if you work or study). Look at Phase 1 on the opposite page. Then the examiner will ask each of you a few DIFFERENT questions (see Phase 2).

Remember

- In Part One, you talk to the examiner, you do not need to talk to your partner.
- Avoid giving one word answers.
- When the examiner asks you about your activities or likes and dislikes extend your answers or give examples.

A DETAILED STUDY

Look at the questions in Phase 2 on the previous page, and at the answers a student gave. Add a sentence so that it is a full answer.

Example:

Question 1:   'Yes, I do.'

Extension: '*I enjoy it very much because the lessons are interesting.*'

Question 2:   'Yes, I think so.'

Extension: '...'

Question 3:   'I went to the cinema.'

Extension: '...'

Question 4:   'Walking.'

Extension: '...'

Check the suggested answers in the key and compare them to your answers.

PART TWO (2–3 minutes)

In this part of the test the examiner will describe a situation and ask you to talk about it with your partner. You will be given a sheet with pictures to help you in your discussion. You will have to talk for about three minutes. The examiner will not take part in the discussion.

This is what the examiner says:

> **I am going to describe a situation to you.**
>
> **A friend of yours is going to live alone in a flat for the first time. You want to give him a present for his new home. Talk together about what you could give him, and then decide which present would be best.**
>
> **Here is a picture with some ideas to help you.**

You may use phrases from the box to help you:

too expensive	we don't know if he's got that/he may have a …
not enough money	somebody gave him a …
he can't cook	this may be very useful
he's already got lots of …	people always give you …

Before doing this part of the test, read the Exam Information and Advice on page 58.

PART THREE (3 minutes)

In Part Three, you will get a colour photograph to describe. You have to give a simple description of what you can see in the photograph and talk for about a minute. Your partner will get a different photograph on the same theme.

This is what the examiner (interlocutor) will say to you:

> **Now I'd like each of you to talk on your own about something. I am going to give each of you a photograph of people learning a skill.**
>
> **Candidate A, here's your photograph. Please show it to Candidate B, but I'd like you to talk about it. Candidate B, you just listen, I'll give you your photograph in a moment.**
>
> **Candidate A, please tell us what you can see in your photograph.**

- *Turn to page 120 and talk about the photograph.*

> **Now, Candidate B, here's your photograph. It also shows people learning a skill. Please show it to Candidate A and tell us what you can see in the photograph.**

- *Turn to page 121 and talk about the photograph.*

Before doing this part of the test, read the Exam Information and Advice on page 87.

PART FOUR (3 minutes)

In Part Four, you and your partner speak together. The examiner (interlocutor) will tell you what you should talk about, and this is always connected with the theme of your photographs in Part Three. This is an opportunity to discuss your experiences, opinions, likes or dislikes with your partner. The examiner will not take part in the discussion.

This is what the examiner will say to you:

> **Your photographs showed people learning a skill. Now, I'd like you to talk together about useful skills you learnt when you were younger and skills that you want to learn in the future.**

After approximately three minutes, the examiner will say:

> **Thank you, that's the end of the test.**

Before doing this part of the test, read the Exam Information and Advice on page 118.

UNIVERSITY *of* **CAMBRIDGE**
ESOL Examinations

Candidate Name
If not already printed, write name
in CAPITALS and complete the
Candidate No. grid (in pencil).

Candidate Signature

Examination Title

Centre

SAMPLE

Supervisor:
If the candidate is ABSENT or has WITHDRAWN shade here ▭

Centre No.

Candidate No.

Examination Details

0	0	0	0
1	1	1	1
2	2	2	2
3	3	3	3
4	4	4	4
5	5	5	5
6	6	6	6
7	7	7	7
8	8	8	8
9	9	9	9

PET Paper 1 Reading and Writing Candidate Answer Sheet 1

Instructions

Use a PENCIL (B or HB).

Rub out any answer you want to change with an eraser.

For **Reading:**
Mark ONE letter for each question.
For example, if you think **A** is the right answer to the
question, mark your answer sheet like this:

Part 1		
1	A B C
2	A B C
3	A B C
4	A B C
5	A B C

Part 2		
6	A B C D E F G H
7	A B C D E F G H
8	A B C D E F G H
9	A B C D E F G H
10	A B C D E F G H

Part 3	
11	A B
12	A B
13	A B
14	A B
15	A B
16	A B
17	A B
18	A B
19	A B
20	A B

Part 4	
21	A B C D
22	A B C D
23	A B C D
24	A B C D
25	A B C D

Part 5	
26	A B C D
27	A B C D
28	A B C D
29	A B C D
30	A B C D
31	A B C D
32	A B C D
33	A B C D
34	A B C D
35	A B C D

Continue on the other side of this sheet ➜

PET RW 1

DP491/389

TEST TWO

PAPER 1: READING 1 hour

PART ONE

Questions 1–5

- Look at the text in each question.
- What does it say?
- Mark the correct letter (**A**, **B** or **C**).

- *In the exam you will mark your answers on a separate sheet (see page 33).*

Example:

0

A   There will be delays on night trains tomorrow.

B   There will be two night trains every hour tomorrow.

C   There will be more night trains from platform 6 tomorrow.

Answer:

1

A   If you find rubbish in the picnic area, tell the manager.

B   You should not leave any rubbish in the picnic area.

C   You must clean the picnic area before using it.

2

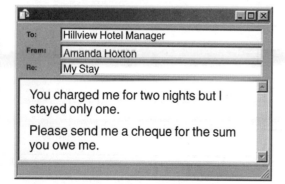

What does Amanda want the manager to do?

A   Change her room booking.

B   Give her a cheaper room.

C   Return some money to her.

3

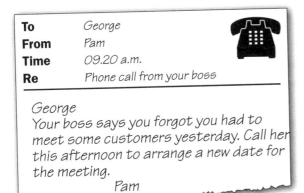

To	George
From	Pam
Time	09.20 a.m.
Re	Phone call from your boss

George
Your boss says you forgot you had to meet some customers yesterday. Call her this afternoon to arrange a new date for the meeting.
                                    Pam

A   George has to telephone his boss.

B   Pam wants to meet George soon.

C   George should see some customers today.

4

Alton Zoo

The monkeys are fed daily at 9.00 a.m.

Visitors are welcome to watch.

A   Visitors can help feed the monkeys at 9.00 a.m.

B   Visitors should never try to feed the monkeys before 9.00 a.m.

C   Visitors can see how the monkeys are fed at 9.00 a.m.

5

NEW HAIRDRESSER

Opening 17th February

Show this advert and get

10% discount.

(Except Saturdays)

A   You can have a haircut every day but not on Saturday.

B   You can pay less for a haircut with this advert.

C   You can get a cheaper haircut only on the opening day.

Before doing this part of the test, read the Exam Information and Advice on page 8.

PART TWO

Questions 6–10

- The people below all want to buy a novel.
- On the opposite page there are descriptions of eight novels.
- Decide which novel would be the most suitable for the following people.
- For questions **6–10**, mark the correct letter (**A–H**).

- *In the exam you will mark your answers on a separate answer sheet (see page 33).*

6

Phil wants to read a thriller. He doesn't travel much, but he wants to read about interesting cities in the world. He is a fast reader, so he wants a long book rather than a short one.

7

Celia only reads novels by well-known authors. She usually likes detective stories, but now she wants to read a romantic novel that will make her cry. She has no patience with long books.

8

Carlos is a Science teacher who likes to read novels about dangerous journeys of the past. He loves books that are based on facts but also have a funny side. He wants a book that has pictures.

9

Thomas is a history student but he wants to read science fiction in his free time. He wants to buy a well-written novel with an unexpected ending.

10

Maria is a primary school teacher and she wants to buy a novel to read on holiday. She would like a novel that describes how children lived in the past.

THIS MONTH'S BESTSELLING NOVELS

A   Difficult Times

Written by a new writer who will one day be famous, this novel tells the story of a 19th century couple and their small sons. We follow them in their daily activities from the day when Neil, the father, loses his job. To enjoy it fully, read it when you have lots of time.

B   Tour of Fear

A young musician is on a tour of Europe when he finds that detectives are following him. Full of danger and excitement, this novel also has wonderful descriptions of the towns where the action takes place. It may take days to read its five-hundred pages, but every minute is enjoyable.

C   No Return

This book is about a man who goes to sleep on a train and wakes up to find himself on another planet. When he meets some strange people, he realizes he can't escape. An interesting story, though you know from the beginning that the story will have a sad ending.

D   Love in the Air

Two women meet on a long bus journey and they start talking. They discover that they have a common childhood friend who is now a well-known writer and decide to go and visit him. What follows is a long romantic story that will make you laugh from beginning to end.

E   A Long Journey

This story takes place in the year 2100. A scientist travels almost a century into the future in a time machine and finds a world where five-year-old children leave home and go to university. You will not be able to guess how it all finishes until the final page!

F   The Mysterious Door

This is another book by the now famous creator of the Detective Brown stories. All the action takes place in a large hotel where the detective is staying. A guest is murdered and everyone is a suspect, including the victim's two grown-up children. The story is sometimes difficult to follow but very enjoyable.

G   All Alone

This thrilling novel takes us back to the eighteenth century. It is the real story of a young man's voyage across the Atlantic in a small ship. This book, which is illustrated with beautiful drawings, will sometimes frighten you and sometimes make you laugh.

H   The Big Adventure

A young woman leaves her home town in search of a better life. This clever love story, which will bring tears to your eyes, is by one of America's most widely-read novelists. Written in a simple style, it can be read in a day but will stay in your memory for a long time.

Before doing this part of the test, read the Exam Information and Advice on the next page.

EXAM INFORMATION AND ADVICE

Part Two tests detailed understanding of factual information. There are five short descriptions of people and eight short texts on the same topic. You have to match each person to one of the texts. There are three texts which you will not need.

1   Read the five descriptions of people and underline the key words.

2   Now read one description and try to find the matching text. The correct text must have all the points that the person requires. For example, if a person wants a romantic book that is short, you must find a text which matches the two requirements: romantic and short.

3   Underline the parts in the text that match the person's description. But be careful about 'word spotting'! It is often not enough to find the same word in the person's description and in the text. It may be the wrong answer. If you find the same word, re-read the person's description and the whole text again carefully.

4   Usually, the correct answer will not contain exactly the same words as the person's description. You may have to recognize different ways of saying the same thing, for example, 'love story' instead of 'romantic', and 'a book I can read quickly' instead of 'a short book'.

5   If you think that there are two texts that seem to match the same person, read the description and the two texts again carefully. Only ONE text will match ALL of a person's requirements.

6   This part of the Reading test cannot be done quickly because you need to read the details in each text carefully, and you may have to go back to a text and re-read it several times. When you are sure you have found an answer, you may want to cross out that particular text as you will not need to read it again.

A DETAILED STUDY

1   Read the extracts from the text on page 36 and answer the questions.

A   *'a novel that describes how **children** lived in the past'* (10 – Maria)
    a)   How many times can you find the word 'children' in texts A–H?
    b)   Are any of them the correct answer to number 10?

B   *'a **romantic** novel that will make her cry'* (7 – Celia)
    a)   In which text, A–H, does the word 'romantic' appear?
    b)   Is it the correct answer to number 7?

2   Link an expression on the left with a similar meaning on the right.

1	thriller	a	journey
2	cities	b	a funny side
3	tears	c	guess
4	takes days	d	easy
5	voyage	e	can't guess
6	know how it will end	f	cry
7	drawings	g	towns
8	widely-read	h	everyday life
9	laugh	i	illustrations
10	can be read quickly	j	long
11	unexpected ending	k	danger and excitement
12	daily activities	l	well-known

Now look at your answers for Part Two and decide if you want to change anything.

PART THREE

Questions 11–20

- Look at the sentences below about a singing group.
- Read the text on the opposite page to decide if each sentence is correct or incorrect.
- If it is correct, mark **A**.
- If it is not correct, mark **B**.

- *In the exam you will mark your answers on a separate answer sheet (see page 33).*

---

11   City Voiceworks has had the same number of members for many years.

12   If you want to become a member of City Voiceworks, you have to pass a test.

13   When you first become a member, you are expected to attend all the practice sessions.

14   You can join City Voiceworks in the first days of September or whenever you want.

15   On 27 March, members will have the opportunity to create their own piece of music.

16   It may be possible to visit other countries with the singing group.

17   The open-air concert will include favourite songs and songs we are not so familiar with.

18   If you want to pay £68 a year, you have to show a document that says you are a student.

19   Everyone must pay a £12 music fee except members who own copies of the sheet music.

20   You are advised to go to the City Voiceworks website rather than phone their Secretary.

Before doing this part of the test, read the Exam Information and Advice on page 68.

CITY VOICEWORKS

Based in the south of England, City Voiceworks is a singing group which has performed in the United Kingdom and in many other countries around the world. It was started nearly 20 years ago and within five years it had grown to around 40 singers. It has continued to grow ever since and it now attracts members from a very wide area who enjoy singing exciting pieces in a pleasant environment. There are no requirements or entrance exams for membership but new members are not allowed to miss practice sessions (Mondays throughout the year except during school holidays). Some knowledge of music is an advantage, though the ability to read music is not necessary in order to become a member. The best time to join is at the beginning of September, but new members are welcome throughout the year.

Special Events this year

27 March
Performing music gives pleasure to everyone, but you can increase your enjoyment when you study music and understand how it is made. In this six-hour class, singers will look at a number of musical pieces and learn how they were created. After the class there will be a group discussion for all participants.

28 to 31 May
Singers will have the opportunity to experience the musical and social delights of touring once again. This annual event has proved very popular with members. Tours both in the UK and abroad have resulted in some fine and memorable performances.

13 June
An open-air concert with the songs everyone knows and enjoys singing, as well as less well-known pieces. The programme, which includes songs from the 14th century to the present day, is designed to have something for all tastes.

Joining Details
Students must bring their college or university card when they register. Members must pay the full annual fee no later than three weeks after joining. If a participant has not paid their fees, a small extra fee may be charged.

A fee of £12 per year is payable by all members to cover the cost of music sheets. This has to be paid even if members have personal copies of the sheets.

We would be delighted to expand on this information, provide details of our music library collection and welcome you to sing with City Voiceworks.

Membership Fees

Full membership
£80 per year (or three payments of £30 each)

Full-time Students
£68 per year (or three payments of £25 each)

Contacts
Please contact the Membership Secretary for further information, Tel. 01228 400460 or visit our website www.cityvoiceworks.co.uk.

PART FOUR

Questions 21–25

- Read the text and questions below.
- For each question, mark the correct letter (**A**, **B**, **C** or **D**).

- *In the exam you will mark your answers on a separate answer sheet (see page 33).*

Sarah Radford, international athlete

'If when you hear the words 'international athlete', you imagine a runner in an exotic location, enjoying life in a five-star hotel, think again. I won the Dublin Marathon and the European Games and I now want to win a place in the Olympic Games. I also have a demanding job and a family life to organize. My life is exciting, but I don't live in luxury.

My route to the top was not what you might expect. I ran until I was sixteen, then went to college and got married. At 25 I made a come-back. That year my daughter was four and although fitting in a full-time job, family and running was not easy, I was managing it all fine. Then I had to stop when I hurt my left knee while running. I started back again a year later, and I'm now running really well.

I am pleased that I am now performing at a high level, but I know that if I make it to the Olympic team there will be more training to do. I may have to decide to work only part-time then, until midday, and get somebody to help with the housework. You have to take an opportunity to compete in the Olympics when it comes because you don't know if it will ever come again.

For the moment, though, training has to fit around everything else in my life. I usually run into work, nearly eight miles along a main road, in my running shoes and tracksuit. Then I quickly change into my work uniform – my employers are used to that! They are also understanding about the demands of life as an athlete, which means I do not work weekends because of races.'

---

21   What is the writer's main purpose in writing the text?

    A   to complain about her lack of time for running

    B   to describe her fitness training programme

    C   to show how difficult being a runner can be

    D   to give advice to other female runners

22   Why did the writer give up running when she was 25?

    A   She had a child to look after.

    B   She suffered an injury.

    C   She wanted to study at college.

    D   She was working full-time.

23 If she joins the Olympic team, the writer is thinking of

   A   training more at weekends.

   B   giving up her present job.

   C   spending more time at home.

   D   reducing her working hours.

24 What does the writer say about her employers?

   A   They allow her free time for running.

   B   They would like her to give up running.

   C   They pay for some of her equipment.

   D   They want her to work weekends.

25 Which of the following is the best description of the writer?

A An athlete who has not won important competitions because of the pressures of family and work.	**B** An excellent runner who has won a number of competitions thanks to a lot of hard work.
C A woman who put her ambition to win competitions before her duties as a mother.	**D** A disappointed runner who would like to have the luxuries that other international athletes have.

Before doing this part of the test, read the Exam Information and Advice on page 98.

PART FIVE

Questions 26–35

- Read the text below and choose the correct word for each space.
- For each question, mark the correct letter (**A**, **B**, **C** or **D**).

- *In the exam you will mark your answers on a separate answer sheet (see page 33).*

Example:

0	**A**	prepared	**B**	organized	**C**	produced	**D**	made

Answer: `0  A  B  C  D`

The Namibia Challenge in Africa

The Namibia Challenge is a seven-day race **(0)** ……………….. by Raleigh International, a company established in 1985. It is a competition for people **(26)** ……………….. want to learn teamwork and communication skills. It **(27)** ……………….. place in the Namib desert in Africa, where teams spend a week pushing themselves to their limit and **(28)** ……………….. useful skills. As a final challenge, participants **(29)** ……………….. to climb Mount Brandberg, Namibia's highest mountain.

Paul Webster, a university student, is willing to **(30)** ……………….. his experiences with other students. 'The Namibia Challenge is especially useful if, **(31)** ……………….. me, you haven't had **(32)** ……………….. experience of working in a team,' he says. '**(33)** ……………….. the end of it, we were all trying to help each other in the team. It is also a great opportunity to **(34)** ……………….. people of many different nationalities in a very special environment. I am **(35)** ……………….. of going back to Namibia if I can.'

26	**A**	what	**B**	which	**C**	who	**D**	whose
27	**A**	takes	**B**	gets	**C**	holds	**D**	has
28	**A**	following	**B**	developing	**C**	growing	**D**	becoming
29	**A**	may	**B**	got	**C**	have	**D**	must
30	**A**	inform	**B**	let	**C**	talk	**D**	share
31	**A**	against	**B**	except	**C**	for	**D**	like
32	**A**	much	**B**	lot	**C**	many	**D**	few
33	**A**	In	**B**	By	**C**	Since	**D**	From
34	**A**	introduce	**B**	meet	**C**	know	**D**	greet
35	**A**	thinking	**B**	planning	**C**	deciding	**D**	considering

PAPER 1: WRITING 30 minutes

PART ONE

Questions 1–5

- Here are some sentences about a new restaurant.
- For each question, complete the second sentence so that it means the same as the first.
- **Use no more than three words.**
- Write only the missing words.

- *In the exam you will write your answers on a separate answer sheet (see page 89).*

Example:

0   The new restaurant's name is The Bluebell.

The name .... **new restaurant is The Bluebell.**

Answer: | **0** | *of the* |

---

1   The owner of The Bluebell is a very rich man.

The new restaurant .... **to a very rich man.**

2   The Bluebell was designed by a famous architect.

A famous architect .... **The Bluebell.**

3   The Bluebell is more comfortable than other restaurants in the area.

Other restaurants in the area are not so .... **The Bluebell.**

4   There are English and French dishes on The Bluebell's menu.

The Bluebell .... **got English and French dishes on its menu.**

5   Meal prices at The Bluebell will change on 30 August.

Meal prices at The Bluebell will be the same .... **30 August.**

Before doing this part of the test, read the Exam Information and Advice on page 18.

PART TWO

Question 6

You are visiting a city and you buy a postcard.

Write the postcard to your English friend Sarah. In your postcard, you should

- explain how you travelled to this city

- say where in the city you are staying

- tell Sarah what you want to do in the city.

Write **35–45 words.**

- *In the exam you will write your answer on a separate answer sheet (see page 89).*

Before doing this part of the test, read the Exam Information and Advice on the next page.

EXAM INFORMATION AND ADVICE

In Part Two, you have to write a short communicative message of between 35 and 45 words. You are told who you have to write to and why. There are always three content points which you must include.

Read the question carefully and plan what you will include. Your message should be clear and it must include all three content points.

Keep to the word limits. Do not write fewer than 35 words. If your answer is very short, it may be that you have missed out one or more of the content points. If your answer is very long, it may be that you have included information that is not required.

A DETAILED STUDY

1   Look at these two answers and answer the questions below.

A

> Dear Sarah
>
> I came to London by plane. I'm staying at the Hilton Hotel. I want to visit some museums here.
>
> Ana

B

> Dear Sarah
>
> The journey was great – I travelled first class on the plane. I am staying at the Hilton Hotel which is very near the shopping and theatre district. Although I am here on business, I also hope to visit some museums.
>
> Love
>
> Ana

a)   Is answer A too short?

b)   Does answer A include all three points?

c)   Is answer B too long?

d)   Does answer B include all three points?

e)   Is answer B better then answer A? Why/Why not?

2   Now look at these two answers to the question. Is something missing?

A

> Dear Sarah
>
> I am in Rome and I am having a great time! My hotel is near Villa Borghese, where there are very beautiful parks. I want to visit a few museums and palaces tomorrow.
>
> Love
>
> Clara

B

> Dear Sarah
>
> I arrived in Rome yesterday, after a lovely journey by train from Venice. Rome is a wonderful city to walk. I'll stay till next week and I want to see everything!
>
> See you soon
>
> Sue

PART THREE
Questions 7–8

Write an answer to **one** of the questions (**7** or **8**).

Write about **100 words**.

Question 7

- This is part of a letter you receive from your English friend Pam.

> I visited the science museum yesterday. It was so interesting! What kind of museums do you like? Are there any good museums near you?

- Now write a letter, answering your friend's questions.
- Write your **letter** in about 100 words.

- *In the exam you will write your answer on a separate answer sheet (see page 89).*

Question 8

- Your English teacher has asked you to write a story.
- Your story must begin with this sentence:

Mark wanted to visit a friend, so he got on a bus.

- Write your **story** in about 100 words.

- *In the exam you will write your answer on a separate answer sheet (see page 89).*

Before you write your letter, read the Exam Information and Advice for Question 7 on page 76.

Before you write your story, read the Exam Information and Advice for Question 8 on page 105.

PAPER 2: LISTENING

PART ONE

Questions 1–7

- There are seven questions in this part.
- For each question there are three pictures and a short recording.
- Choose the correct picture and put a tick (✔) in the box below it.

- *In the exam you will write your answers on the question paper and then you will have six minutes to copy them on to the answer sheet (see page 119).*

Example: Which musical instrument will the man buy?

A ✔   B ☐   C ☐

---

1   At what time will the art gallery open this weekend?

A ☐   B ☐   C ☐

2   What will the woman order for lunch?

A ☐   B ☐   C ☐

3 Where did the man find the handbag?

A ☐   B ☐   C ☐

4 How did the man get to his office yesterday?

A ☐   B ☐   C ☐

5 What piece of furniture do they decide to buy first?

A ☐   B ☐   C ☐

6   What will they do on Saturday afternoon?

A ☐   **B** ☐   **C** ☐

7   What's the weather like at the seaside today?

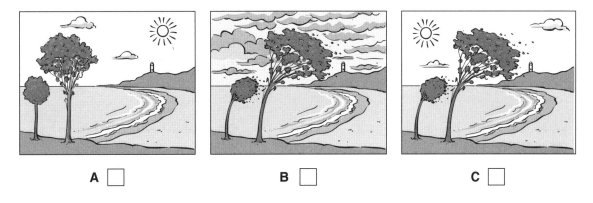

A ☐   **B** ☐   **C** ☐

Before doing this part of the test, read the Exam Information and Advice on page 24.

PART TWO

Questions 8–13

- You will hear a man called Patrick Simmons talking on the radio about his career as a chef.
- For each question, put a tick (✔) in the correct box.

- *In the exam you will write your answers on the question paper and then you will have six minutes to copy them on to the answer sheet (see page 119).*

---

8   Patrick accepted his first job as a chef because

    A   his mother wanted him to do it. ☐

    B   it would help him in his studies. ☐

    C   he had to earn some money. ☐

9   What did Patrick dislike about his job at the hotel?

    A   The menu seldom changed. ☐

    B   The manager was unfriendly. ☐

    C   The working hours were long. ☐

10   What does Patrick say about his Italian restaurant job?

    A   Other Italian restaurants copied his recipes. ☐

    B   He managed to reduce costs for the owner. ☐

    C   The restaurant's owner created some menus. ☐

11   Patrick thinks that his best recipes are for

    A   chicken. ☐

    B   vegetables. ☐

    C   bread. ☐

12   According to Patrick, what are chefs often unable to do?

    A   listen to others ☐

    B   create original dishes ☐

    C   use the latest technology ☐

13   What does Patrick advise students to do?

    A   to look for a part-time job ☐

    B   to concentrate only on their studies ☐

    C   to talk to experienced chefs ☐

Before doing this part of the test, read the Exam Information and Advice on the next page.

EXAM INFORMATION AND ADVICE

In Part Two, you listen to a longer text which can either be a monologue, e.g. Test Three, or an interview with questions from a radio presenter. It will either be an informative text about places or events, or somebody talking about his/her life, or job. You have to answer six multiple-choice questions as you listen to the text. You will hear the text twice.

Prepare yourself for listening by using the information you have on the page:

- Read the instructions for the task. They tell you who you will hear and what they will be talking about. Think of what you know about the subject and of the words you might hear. You will understand more if you activate the vocabulary you know.

- Next, read the six questions and their options quickly to get a general idea of the points that will be mentioned.

Concentrate on each question as you listen:

- During the first listening, try to understand the general meaning and choose the best option. Remember the questions follow the order of the interview, and if you miss something you can always get it when you hear it a second time, so keep calm.

- During the second listening, pay attention to the more detailed meaning and check your answers carefully.

A DETAILED STUDY

1   Before you listen to the recording, read through the questions and their options A, B and C. Which of the statements a–g can you say are True or False without listening to the recording?

		True	False
a)	Patrick was offered a job as a chef.	☐	☐
b)	Patrick enjoyed every aspect of his hotel job.	☐	☐
c)	Patrick was unhappy about working late at the hotel.	☐	☐
d)	At the Italian restaurant, Patrick asked the owner to create some menus.	☐	☐
e)	Patrick thinks that all his recipes are equally good.	☐	☐
f)	Patrick says some chefs create boring dishes.	☐	☐
g)	Patrick gives advice to students.	☐	☐

2   Listen to the recording once only and answer these general questions about the interview.

- a)   Why did Patrick's mother want him to go to Cooking School?
- b)   What made the hotel manager unhappy?
- c)   What did Patrick manage to do at the Italian restaurant?
- d)   What does Patrick say about his chicken recipes?
- e)   According to Patrick, how many chefs keep up-to-date with technological developments?
- f)   As well as studying, what else should students do while at Cooking School?

Now you are ready to listen to Part Two again and answer questions 8–13.

PART THREE

Questions 14–19

- You will hear a tourist guide talking to a group of people about a trip to the countryside.
- For each question, fill in the missing information in the numbered space.

- *In the exam you will write your answers on the question paper and then you will have six minutes to copy them on to the answer sheet (see page 119).*

A DAY IN THE COUNTRYSIDE

Morning programme:

- breakfast at 8.30

- meet in **(14)** ....

- bus leaves at: **(15)** ....

- picnic lunch in the **(16)** ....

Afternoon programme:

Choice of activities:

- hill walk

- visit to a **(17)** .... or a farm

- swim or take a trip by **(18)** ....

What to bring:

- a warm jacket

- a **(19)** ....

Before doing this part of the test, read the Exam Information and Advice on page 82.

PART FOUR

Questions 20–25

- Look at the six sentences for this part.
- You will hear a conversation between a man, James, and a woman, Diana, about taking photographs.
- Decide if each sentence is correct or incorrect.
- If it is correct, put a tick (✔) in the box under **A** for **YES**. If it is not correct, put a tick (✔) in the box under **B** for **NO**.

- *In the exam you will write your answers on the question paper and then you will have six minutes to copy them on to the answer sheet (see page 119).*

		A **YES**	**B** **NO**
20	When taking photos, Diana avoids getting close to wild animals.	☐	☐
21	James thinks that everybody can take good photos with a good camera.	☐	☐
22	Diana's parents are happy for her to take up photography as a career.	☐	☐
23	James was surprised how easy it was to take underwater photographs.	☐	☐
24	Diana suggests someone who can give James lessons on underwater photography.	☐	☐
25	James persuades Diana to take some photos at the school party.	☐	☐

Before doing this part of the test, read the Exam Information and Advice on page 113.

SPEAKING

PART ONE (2–3 minutes)

In Part One the examiner (interlocutor) will ask each of you some personal questions – your name, where you live, about your work or studies, about your free time activities, etc. The questions can be about the past, the present or the future.

Preliminary English Test
Speaking Test

Part 1 (2–3 minutes)

Phase 1
Interlocutor

A/B   Good morning / afternoon / evening.
Can I have your mark sheets, please?

A/B   I'm .... and this is ....
He/she is just going to listen to us.

A   Now, what's your name?
Thank you.

B   And, what's your name?
Thank you.

Back-up prompts

B
| What's your surname? | How do you write your family/second |
| How do you spell it? | name? |

Thank you.

A   And, what's your surname?
How do you spell it?

Thank you.

(Ask the following questions. Ask A first)

Where do you live / come from?

Do you work or are you a student in ...?
What do you do / study?

Thank you.
(Repeat for B)

Do you live in ...?

Have you got a job?
What job do you do? / What subject(s) do you study?

Now answer these Phase 2 questions, paying attention to the verb tense you use. Remember to extend your answers (see Exam Information and Advice, page 29).

- *What will you do next Saturday?*
- *How often do you go to the cinema?*
- *What is your favourite food?*
- *What do you like doing in the evenings?*
- *Do you like using computers? Why (not)?*
- *Where did you go for your holidays last summer?*

PART TWO (2–3 minutes)

In this part of the test the examiner will describe a situation and ask you to talk about it with your partner. You will be given a sheet with pictures to help you in your discussion. You will have to talk for about three minutes. The examiner will not take part in the discussion.

This is what the examiner says:

> **I am going to describe a situation to you.**
>
> **A friend of yours wants to spend a year in an English-speaking country studying English and doing a part-time job. Talk together about the different jobs she could do, and then decide which one would be best for practising her English.**
>
> **Here is a picture with some ideas to help you.**

Before doing this part of the test, read the Exam Information and Advice on the next page.

EXAM INFORMATION AND ADVICE

Part Two is a collaborative/discussion task.

Listen to the task carefully, paying attention to the second part: *and then decide* …

First, talk about the different ideas (the 5 or 6 pictures around the central image), and after that, decide which idea is best.

1   How to start

Shall we talk about this picture first?

OK, let's start with this one, shall we?

Shall I go first? I think …

2   How to give an opinion

In my opinion, …

I am sure that …

I think/ believe that …

3   How to ask for your partner's opinion

What do you think?

Do you agree with me?

What's your opinion?

4   How to agree with your partner

I think you're right.

I agree with what you said.

Absolutely.

5   How to disagree with your partner

I'm afraid I disagree with that.

I don't think so.

I have a different opinion.

6   How to move on to the decision
(second part of the question):

So, which one is best?

Shall we decide which is best now?

I think we agree that X is the best, don't we?

Remember to:

ask your partner's opinions.

give reasons for your opinions.

listen to what your partner says and respond to it.

Remember NOT to:

describe each picture, this is a discussion.

start by answering the second part of the task (decide). You may run out of things to say.

A DETAILED STUDY

Look at the following opinions and at the visual images on page 57. Imagine the following opinions are your partner's. Reply to each one, starting with:

You're absolutely right …
OR
Yes, that's true but …
OR
I don't think so. In my opinion …

You can use the ideas in the boxes.

1   *I think a job as a waitress is good because she will be able to talk to lots of different people. She has to understand what the customers say and she has to explain the dishes on the menu.*

> **Ideas:** customers may not speak English/she only talks about food

2   *This is a good job for her. Working in a hotel carrying suitcases is hard work but she may get a lot of tips and meet many people at the hotel. What do you think?*

> **Ideas:** no chance to talk to the people who arrive/she may be very tired after this job/won't feel like doing her English homework

3   *Looking after children is a good job. She will learn English from the children and from their parents. She may also have time to read while the children play on their own.*

> **Ideas:** You have to be very patient, children may be difficult/she won't see the parents because they may be working

PART THREE (3 minutes)

In Part Three, you will get a colour photograph to describe. You have to give a simple description of what you can see in the photograph and talk for about a minute. Your partner will get a different photograph on the same theme.

This is what the examiner (interlocutor) will say to you:

> **Now I'd like each of you to talk on your own about something. I am going to give each of you a photograph of people having a meal.**
>
> **Candidate A, here's your photograph. Please show it to Candidate B, but I'd like you to talk about it. Candidate B, you just listen, I'll give you your photograph in a moment.**
>
> **Candidate A, please tell us what you can see in your photograph.**

● *Turn to page 122 and talk about the photograph.*

> **Now, Candidate B, here's your photograph. It also shows people having a meal. Please show it to Candidate A and tell us what you can see in the photograph.**

● *Turn to page 123 and talk about the photograph.*

Before doing this part of the test, read the Exam Information and Advice on page 87.

PART FOUR (3 minutes)

In Part Four, you and your partner speak together. The examiner (interlocutor) will tell you what you should talk about, and this is always connected with the theme of your photographs in Part Three. This is an opportunity to discuss your experiences, opinions, likes or dislikes with your partner. The examiner will not take part in the discussion.

This is what the examiner will say to you:

> **Your photographs showed people having a meal. Now, I'd like you to talk together about your favourite meals and how you prepare them or cook them.**

After approximately three minutes, the examiner will say:

> **Thank you, that's the end of the test.**

Before doing this part of the test, read the Exam Information and Advice on page 118.

TEST THREE

PAPER 1: READING 1 hour

PART ONE

Questions 1–5

- Look at the text in each question.
- What does it say?
- Mark the correct letter (**A**, **B** or **C**).

- *In the exam you will mark your answers on a separate sheet (see page 33).*

Example:

0

A   There will be delays on night trains tomorrow.

B   There will be two night trains every hour tomorrow.

C   There will be more night trains from platform 6 tomorrow.

Answer:

1

Monday, 12.30
Alan
Your dentist called. Your appointment tomorrow will be at 6.30 instead of 5.30. If that's no good for you, call her today.
Janet

A   Alan must phone Janet to find out more about his appointment.

B   Alan needs to call his dentist if he can't make the new appointment.

C   Alan's dentist wants to change the date of his appointment.

2

A   If you wish to smoke, go to the smoking area of the train.

B   You are requested not to smoke anywhere except in the toilets.

C   You cannot smoke anywhere while on board the train.

3

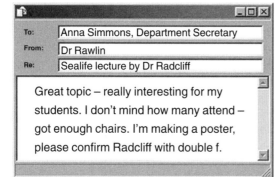

To: Anna Simmons, Department Secretary

From: Dr Rawlin

Re: Sealife lecture by Dr Radcliff

Great topic – really interesting for my students. I don't mind how many attend – got enough chairs. I'm making a poster, please confirm Radcliff with double f.

Dr Rawlin needs more information about

A the number of students.

B the name of the lecturer.

C the topic of the lecture.

4

PLEASE GIVE UP YOUR SEAT TO PEOPLE CARRYING CHILDREN.

A You can only use this seat if you are carrying children.

B People carrying children are requested to remain seated.

C If somebody carrying a child gets on, offer them your seat.

5

CUSTOMER OFFER
BUY TWO OF OUR
LARGE CAKES AND GET A
THIRD SMALL ONE
FREE!

A When you buy two large cakes, we charge you for only one of them.

B We give you a small free cake with every large cake you buy.

C If you pay for two large cakes, we give you a small one as a present.

PART TWO

Questions 6–10

- The people below are all on holiday.
- On the opposite page there are descriptions of eight tourist attractions.
- Decide which attraction would be the most suitable for the following people.
- For questions **6–10**, mark the correct letter (**A–H**).

- *In the exam you will mark your answers on a separate answer sheet (see page 33).*

6

Simon hasn't got a car and he wants a day out in an area of natural beauty. He would like to see wild animals but does not approve of keeping them in cages.

7

Alice is a student and wants to combine a walk in the open air with a visit to an art exhibition. She also wants to buy a present for a friend.

8

David is a Biology teacher. He is going back home on Monday afternoon but has time in the morning. He also wants to get something that he may use in class with his students.

9

Marcia is a student and wants to learn more about the effects of climate changes on planet earth. She would like to attend an interesting talk about this.

10

Jon wants an activity for Saturday. He is interested in how artists work. He wants to see them at work rather than just see the finished product. He also wants to buy something for his house.

TOURIST ATTRACTIONS

A   The World of Glass

Admire the skills of our glass makers and watch them while they turn liquid glass into beautiful objects! The colours and shapes of their pieces are inspired by the local landscape and wildlife. After your visit, buy a unique vase for your home. Open weekends only, 9.00–5.00.

B   South Lakes Conservation Park

See animals from all over the world living free in open fields and learn how we protect them when their environment is damaged by human beings. You will need a day to see everything, so bring lunch and use our picnic areas set in wonderful surroundings! Easy access by public transport.

C   The Mountain Exhibition

This exhibition tells the story of mountains before, during and after the Ice Age and how the wildlife on them adapted to survive. There are audio-visual shows and lectures by experts one hour before closing time every day. Open every afternoon from 1.00 to 7.00.

D   Sculpture Garden

Come and see some of the most beautiful modern sculptures in the world. We have works by Henry Moore and many other famous sculptors from Africa, Europe and South America. The sculptures, which are not for sale, are set in a lovely garden among local species of trees and wild flowers. We have a large tree car park.

E   Lancaster Castle and Gardens

Built in the13th century, the Castle has valuable collections of paintings, books and furniture on display. Make sure you give yourself plenty of time to tour the gardens, with ancient trees which are home to varied bird life. In our Visitor Shop you can get great gifts for all tastes.

F   Sandow Zoo

Sandow Zoo, in the heart of the city, is open every day except Mondays from 10 a.m. to 5 p.m. You are invited to share the excitement of zoo life and watch the keepers feeding the lions and tigers! Please see our website for details of special talks for school children.

G   Waterworld Centre

1.4 million litres of sea water with a viewing window and an underwater gallery to make you feel you are at the bottom of the ocean. See amazing marine creatures and sea plants, and buy an informative video on your way out. Visits every day 9–11 a.m. or 4–6 p.m. Close to the bus station.

H   The Railway Museum

Imagine yourself back in time, travelling through lovely countryside in a train … At the Railway Museum you can experience the sights, sounds and even the smell of the trains of the nineteenth century. This is an unforgettable day for the whole family. Open at weekends all year round.

PART THREE
Questions 11–20

- Look at the sentences below about holidays in New Zealand.
- Read the text on the opposite page to decide if each sentence is correct or incorrect.
- If it is correct, mark **A**.
- If it is not correct, mark **B**.

- *In the exam you will mark your answers on a separate answer sheet (see page 33).*

---

11 Programme 1 requires the ability to walk without stopping for no less than two hours.

12 In Programme 1, you can take part in research to improve conditions for local birds.

13 In Programme 1, you can choose between accommodation in people's houses or in forest cabins.

14 In Programme 2, you will visit an area that New Zealand people do not know.

15 All activities in Programme 2 will take place whatever the weather conditions.

16 For Programme 2, participants must bring waterproof equipment with them.

17 You should send the application form after you have checked that there is a place available for you.

18 After you have paid the deposit, you get your money back if you cancel your booking.

19 You must pay the programme fee no later than the day you arrive in New Zealand.

20 The programme organizers can get travel insurance for you at an additional cost.

Before doing this part of the test, read the Exam Information and Advice on page 68.

NEW ZEALAND ADVENTURES

Do you want to see the beauty of New Zealand and have
an unforgettable experience? Then choose
one of these programmes ...

Programme 1:

Nature in New Zealand

New Zealand's native wildlife is unique and this programme covers a large area, so in six days, many sites can be visited and a lot can be seen. Participants need to have a medium level of fitness and be able to walk for at least two hours at a time during a normal six-hour trek.

  The native forests are home to unique bird life. Participants in this programme will not only learn about projects to improve the area for the birds but they will also have an opportunity to work on the projects, helped by local scientific researchers.

  Participants will stay with local New Zealanders who have deep knowledge of the natural environment and who will give them a bed for the night and breakfast in their own homes. During the course of the programme, there will also be a walk through native forest on an overnight guided trip, staying in basic but comfortable bush cabins built in the forest.

Programme 2:

Wild New Zealand

New Zealand has sharp contrasts in its geography, and this programme focuses on the wild landscape of an area which is little known outside of New Zealand: the Wellington and Wairarapa regions. Here participants will leave the main path and take part in some exciting activities to get closer to nature. Depending on the weather, the programme will include white water rafting, visiting caves and mountain walks. Most of the places visited are very rough, wet and muddy. Waterproof jackets and strong boots are essential items which cannot be bought locally.

Application Process

1   Complete and send us the application form. Upon receipt of the form we will check the availability we have for the programme you have chosen. We will then either email you a letter of acceptance or suggest other available programmes.

2   Decision point: Once you have read through the letter of acceptance, it is time to pay your deposit to secure your place on the programme. Please note that we will return your deposit if you decide not to go after all.

3   When you have paid your deposit, we will send you an eight-page booklet with further details about the programme you have chosen, including the arrangements to welcome you on arrival. The full programme fee covers airport pick up, accommodation, meals and guiding and needs to be paid to us eight weeks before you start the programme. You will need to pay for other costs, such as taxes, and to arrange your own travel insurance for the whole of your journey, as we do not provide that service.

EXAM INFORMATION AND ADVICE

Part Three tests your ability to read a longer text and look for factual information. You have to find practical information in a leaflet, an advertisement, a website, a holiday brochure, etc.

There are ten sentences about the text. The sentences will follow the order of the text. You must read each sentence and decide if it is correct or incorrect according to the text.

First, read the whole text quickly to get a general understanding of what it is about. Then read a sentence and read the text to find the part that has the answer. Then re-read that part of the text very carefully. You do not need to re-read the whole text carefully, only the parts that have answers to questions. Part Three is the longest text in the test, but it has lots of information you will not need.

In Part Three, you may find some words you do not know. You do not need to understand every word to answer the questions correctly. Just concentrate on getting the information you require to answer the question and do not worry about unfamiliar words.

A DETAILED STUDY

In order to answer the questions, you have to decide if the sentence says the same as the text. You need to look at the sentence and the text very carefully. Sometimes the words look similar, but the meaning is different.

What is the meaning of these phrases? Tick (✔) a or b.

1   *walk for up to two hours at a time during a normal six-hour trek.*

    a)   You can stop and have a break after two hours, and then again after the next two hours.

    b)   You can have just one long two-hour break during a normal six-hour walk.

2   *participants will not only … but also …*

    a)   Participants will choose between two things.

    b)   Participants will be able to do both things.

3   *… an overnight guided trip, staying in forest cabins …*

    a)   Participants on the overnight guided trip will stay in forest cabins.

    b)   Participants on the overnight guided trip may prefer to stay in forest cabins.

4   *an area … little known outside of New Zealand*

    a)   People in other countries hardly know about this area.

    b)   New Zealand people do not know about this area.

5   *depending on the weather*

    a)   We hope the weather is suitable.

    b)   If the weather is suitable …

6   *essential items which cannot be bought locally*

    a)   You are not able to buy these items here.

    b)   Local people may be able to get these items.

7   *Upon receipt of the form we will check X …*

    a)   We will check X before we receive the form.

    b)   We will check X after we receive the form.

8   *if you decide not to go after all*

    a)   … if we decide to cancel your booking.

    b)   … if you change your mind about going.

9   *needs to be paid to us*

    a)   You need this money from us.

    b)   We need to receive this money from you.

10   *… to arrange your own travel insurance …*

    a)   to be responsible for your travel insurance

    b)   to ask the programme organizers about your travel insurance

Check your answers to the Detailed Study section.

Now look at your answers to Part Three again and decide if you want to change anything.

PART FOUR

Questions 21–25

- Read the text and questions below.
- For each question, mark the correct letter (**A, B, C** or **D**).

- *In the exam you will mark your answers on a separate answer sheet (see page 33).*

SUMMER JOBS FOR STUDENTS

Employers are more and more interested in taking on students during their holiday periods. Students can do the easier tasks and free up time for their permanent employees to concentrate on the more demanding ones. Although there is little financial reward for students, it is a great chance to explore their interests and add to their CVs. However, few students know what jobs may be available.

Colleges sometimes advertise summer jobs on their notice-boards and in newspapers, and there are also well-known international organizations which can help. Students can also search the web, find an interesting company and email the manager to ask what temporary jobs exist. This may sound time-consuming, but students then get to work in the company of their choice, so it is what I recommend.

As a science student, two years ago I spent ten weeks in a laboratory in California, helping a group of researchers with their work. To begin with, the job seemed uninteresting because my responsibilities were not clear, but when I started working on a range of projects, such as writing research papers and creating web pages, my attitude changed.

I was paid enough to cover all my daily needs, so I had no financial worries. One of my jobs was to prepare educational material for schools. This was an entirely new challenge which I enjoyed so much that I decided to train as a teacher rather than a researcher when I got back. My only regret was that I'd been too busy to learn more about the USA, but then a good summer job seldom leaves you much free time and you should be prepared for that.

21   What is the writer's main purpose in writing the text?

    A   to warn students about low-paid summer jobs

    B   to describe the best summer jobs for students

    C   to encourage students to look for summer jobs

    D   to offer students interesting summer jobs

22   The writer says the best way to find a good summer job is

    A   to ask their own colleges for help.

    B   to read the job advertisements in the press.

    C   to join an organized student programme.

    D   to contact possible employers directly.

23 The writer found the California job disappointing at first because

A he was not sure what he had to do.

B he had to work on too many projects.

C he did not like research work.

D he lacked good computer skills.

24 In what way did the California job benefit the writer?

A It allowed him to save some money.

B It gave him contacts he could use later.

C It made him change his career plans.

D It taught him what life was like in the USA.

25 Which of these could be the writer speaking?

A A summer job is a good way of getting to see the world.

B Students are often unaware of summer job opportunities.

C Employers are unwilling to offer summer jobs to students.

D Students should be better paid for doing summer jobs.

PART FIVE

Questions 26–35

- Read the text below and choose the correct word for each space.
- For each question, mark the correct letter (**A**, **B**, **C** or **D**).

- *In the exam you will mark your answers on a separate sheet (see page 33).*

Example:

| 0 | **A** | partner | **B** | member | **C** | part | **D** | person |

Answer: 0 A **B** C D

Beatrice Wright, a Storyteller

Beatrice is a retired librarian and a **(0)** ……………….. of The Storytellers, a group of people who

(26) ……………….. into schools to read with children. The Storytellers are volunteers, so they are not

(27) ……………….. for their work. There are now almost 3,000 storytellers of all **(28)** ………………..

across Great Britain, from young students to people in their seventies. **(29)** ………………..

qualifications at all are needed to be a storyteller, but all storytellers **(30)** ……………….. be patient and

kind.

Beatrice applied to **(31)** ……………….. a storyteller when she saw an advertisement on TV. She had

never **(32)** ……………….. of The Storytellers before. She says, ' Many children do not have books at

home and this **(33)** ……………….. it harder for them to do well at school. They are delighted when they

get all my attention. People should not do this sort of work **(34)** ……………….. they really like children.

I look forward to it so much that I really **(35)** ……………….. the children during the holidays.'

26	**A**	appear	**B**	attend	**C**	visit	**D**	go
27	**A**	charged	**B**	paid	**C**	owed	**D**	fined
28	**A**	ages	**B**	years	**C**	times	**D**	dates
29	**A**	None	**B**	Nothing	**C**	No	**D**	Any
30	**A**	ought	**B**	need	**C**	must	**D**	have
31	**A**	train	**B**	turn	**C**	work	**D**	become
32	**A**	heard	**B**	told	**C**	informed	**D**	listened
33	**A**	means	**B**	makes	**C**	does	**D**	gets
34	**A**	if	**B**	though	**C**	unless	**D**	even
35	**A**	lose	**B**	lack	**C**	leave	**D**	miss

PAPER 1: WRITING 30 minutes

PART ONE

Questions 1–5

- Here are some sentences about a school.
- For each question, complete the second sentence so that it means the same as the first.
- **Use no more than three words.**
- Write only the missing words.

- *In the exam you will write your answers on a separate answer sheet (see page 89).*

Example:

0   The King School has been open for five years.

The King School .... **five years ago.**

Answer: | 0 | *opened* |

---

1   Last year the King School had more than 500 students.

Last year there .... **more than 500 students at the King School.**

2   I asked at Reception about the price of a conversation course.

I asked at Reception: 'How much .... **a conversation course cost?'**

3   The coursebook is included in the price of the course.

The price of the course .... **the coursebook.**

4   All the other schools in town are more expensive than the King School.

The King School is the .... **expensive of all schools in town.**

5   Students are not allowed to attend classes if they have not paid the fee.

Students are not allowed to attend classes .... **they have paid the fee.**

PART TWO
Question 6

An English friend of yours called Peter has sent you a picture as a present.

Write a card to send to Peter. In your card, you should:

- thank Peter for the present

- say what you will do with the present

- suggest when Peter could visit you.

Write **35–45 words.**

- *In the exam you will write your answer on a separate answer sheet (see page 89).*

PART THREE
Questions 7–8

Write an answer to **one** of the questions (**7** or **8**).

Write about **100 words**.

Question 7

- This is part of a letter you receive from your English penfriend.

> *I have a new hobby – collecting stamps.*
> *Have you ever collected things? Tell me*
> *about your favourite hobby.*

- Now write a letter to your penfriend about your favourite hobby.
- Write your **letter** in about 100 words.

- *In the exam you will write your answer on a separate answer sheet (see page 89).*

Question 8

- You want to write a story for a competition in a magazine.
- This is the title for your story:

The castle on the hill

- Write your story in about 100 words.

- *In the exam you will write your answer on a separate answer sheet (see page 89).*

Before doing this part of the test, read the Exam Information and Advice on the next page.

EXAM INFORMATION AND ADVICE

In Part Three, you have a choice of task: either an informal letter or a story of about 100 words.

The informal letter

You get an extract of a letter from a friend of yours. Read this extract carefully because it gives you the topic you must write about. Use the questions in the extract to focus your ideas. Remember that you must keep to the topic.

Try to write at least 90 words and don't worry if your answer is a bit longer than 100 words. Your answer should not be under 80 words.

In this part, you will get better marks if you use different tenses, vocabulary and expressions. Use the language you know and don't be afraid of making mistakes.

When you have finished, check your spelling and grammar.

A DETAILED STUDY

1   Look at this list of ideas for the letter. Put a tick (✔) next to the ones you think are on the topic and a cross (✗) next to the ones that are not on the topic.

a)   a TV programme about hobbies

b)   how I started collecting something

c)   how often I practise my hobby

d)   why I don't have any hobbies

e)   why I enjoy my hobby

f)   my sister's hobbies

g)   who I practise my hobby with

h)   how expensive my hobby is

i)   how I spend my free time

j)   playing computer games

2   Now read this sample answer. It is only 75 words. Add the sentences A, B and C below in spaces 1, 2 and 3 to make it longer.

> Dear Jack
> I was really pleased to get your letter. Collecting stamps must be very interesting. I also like collecting things. When I was a child I used to collect toy cars. **1** ....
> My favourite hobby now is making model aeroplanes. It is great fun, but it is not easy. **2** .... I have to be careful because they break very easily. I keep them in my bedroom on special shelves.
> **3** ....
> Write again soon
> Yours
> Daniel

A   You get the parts with the instructions and you have to put them all together.

B   Shall I send you some photographs of my planes?

C   I still have them and they look like new, though they are very old.

PAPER 2: LISTENING

PART ONE

Questions 1–7

- There are seven questions in this part.
- For each question there are three pictures and a short recording.
- Choose the correct picture and put a tick (✔) in the box below it.

- *In the exam you will write your answers on the question paper and then you will have six minutes to copy them on to the answer sheet (see page 119).*

Example: Which musical instrument will the man buy?

A ✔

B ☐

C ☐

---

1   What present do they decide to give their uncle?

A ☐

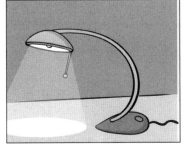

B ☐

C ☐

2   What does Margaret look like now?

A ☐

B ☐

C ☐

3   Where will they have the party?

       A ☐   **B** ☐   **C** ☐

4   Which magazine does the woman read regularly?

       A ☐   **B** ☐   **C** ☐

5   Which music event is free?

       A ☐   **B** ☐   **C** ☐

6   At what time will Brenda phone Jackie tomorrow?

A ☐   B ☐   C ☐

7   What was the boy doing when the lights went off?

A ☐   B ☐   C ☐

PART TWO
Questions 8–13

- You will hear a radio presenter reviewing this weekend's evening television programmes.
- For each question, put a tick (✔) in the correct box.

- *In the exam you will write your answers on the question paper and then you will have six minutes to copy them on to the answer sheet (see page 119).*

---

8   *Wildlife of Madagascar* is disappointing because

   A   it is not colourful enough.   ☐

   B   it was filmed in a tourist area.   ☐

   C   it shows few interesting animals.   ☐

9   The drama series *Last Witness*

   A   has a surprising ending.   ☐

   B   has been on TV too long.   ☐

   C   has both good and bad actors.   ☐

10   *The Bill Smith Show*

   A   has a new actor.   ☐

   B   used to be better.   ☐

   C   is for adults only.   ☐

11   *Men of Iron*, the history programme,

   A   will start at an earlier time.   ☐

   B   has changed to another channel.   ☐

   C   took a long time to film.   ☐

12   *Secret Job* is recommended because

   A   it is about a real person.   ☐

   B   the story is original.   ☐

   C   the actors are good.   ☐

13   What is the problem with *Student Life*?

   A   It has only female characters.   ☐

   B   The stories are not exciting enough.   ☐

   C   There is too much about city life.   ☐

PART THREE
Questions 14–19

- You will hear a teacher talking to a group of people about evening leisure courses in a college.
- For each question, fill in the missing information in the numbered space.

- *In the exam you will write your answers on the question paper and then you will have six minutes to copy them on to the answer sheet (see page 119).*

EVENING LEISURE COURSES
at Lancaster College

Length:	3 months or 6 months
Classes once a week on:	**(14)** ....…………........ from 6 to 9 p.m.
Place:	College building opposite the **(15)** ....………….......

Three-month courses:

starting on: **(16)** ....…………........

- *Play an instrument*
  (either the piano or the **(17)** ....…………........)

- *Painting for Beginners*

Six-month courses:

- *Modern Dance*

- *What makes a good* **(18)** ....…………....... *?*

Fees: 60 euros (three months)

150 euros (six months)

(19) ....…………....... not included.

Before doing this part of the test, read the Exam Information and Advice on the next page.

EXAM INFORMATION AND ADVICE

In Part Three you listen to a longer monologue which provides information about places or events (trips, holiday activities, courses, etc). It may be a radio announcement or an extract from a talk or radio programme. On the page, there are notes (as in Tests One, Two and Three) or incomplete sentences (as in Test Four) with six gaps. As you listen, you have to fill in the gaps with words from the text. In the recording you will hear the exact word you need to write. You need to write only one or two words in each gap.

1   Read the instructions carefully. They tell you about the context and the speaker.

2   Read the notes or sentences before the recording starts. Think of the information and the language you are going to hear. This will help you to feel prepared for the answers when the recording starts.

3   Try to decide whether you are listening for a name, number, date, address, etc.

4   Remember this is not a dictation test, so the words before the gaps are not usually the same words you will hear! You have to listen for the meaning of the text in order to locate the information you need.

5   Remember that you will also hear information which you do not need.

6   While you listen, use the information on the page to guide you through the text.

7   If you are not sure about an answer during the first listening, remember you will hear the piece twice, so don't worry.

8   Check your final answers (including spelling) and be careful when you transfer the words on to the answer sheet.

A DETAILED STUDY

When working on exercises 1 and 2 below, you will need to refer back to Part Three, questions 14–19.

1   Before you look at the notes or listen to Part Three, read the instructions carefully. What do they tell you about what you are going to hear?

   a)   Who is the person speaking?

   b)   What is the subject?

   c)   Can you imagine what sort of information the speaker will give? (programme, prices, etc.)

2   Now read the notes and choose from the list below what you will need for each gap:

a)	the name of a job or object	**f)**	a price
b)	the name of an object(s)	**g)**	a year
c)	a date	**h)**	the name of an instrument
d)	the name of a place or city	**i)**	an address
e)	a building	**j)**	a day of the week

Check your answers. Now listen to the recording and fill in the gaps (14–19).

PART FOUR

Questions 20–25

- Look at the six sentences for this part.
- You will hear a conversation between a girl, Nora, and a boy, Sam, about working in an office.
- Decide if each sentence is correct or incorrect.
- If it is correct, put a tick (✔) in the box under **A** for **YES**. If it is not correct, put a tick (✔) in the box under **B** for **NO**.

- *In the exam you will write your answers on the question paper and then you will have six minutes to copy them on to the answer sheet (see page 119).*

		A YES	B NO
20	Nora is doubtful about whether to apply for an office job.	☐	☐
21	Sam found his experience of working in an office useful.	☐	☐
22	Sam dislikes the idea of spending many hours working with a computer.	☐	☐
23	Sam believes that Nora's knowledge of German is better than his.	☐	☐
24	Nora and Sam agree about the importance of finding a well-paid job.	☐	☐
25	Nora accepts Sam's offer to help her search the Internet for jobs.	☐	☐

PAPER 3: SPEAKING

PART ONE (2–3 minutes)

In Part One the examiner (interlocutor) will ask each of you some personal questions – your name, where you live, about your work or studies, about your free time activities, etc. The questions can be about the past, the present or the future.

Preliminary English Test
Speaking Test

Part 1 (2–3 minutes)

Phase 1
Interlocutor

A/B	**Good morning / afternoon / evening.** **Can I have your mark sheets, please?**	
A/B	**I'm .... and this is ....** **He/she is just going to listen to us.**	
A	**Now, what's your name?** **Thank you.**	
B	**And, what's your name?** **Thank you.**	***Back-up prompts***

B	**What's your surname?** **How do you spell it?** **Thank you.**	**How do you write your family/second name?**
A	**And, what's your surname?** **How do you spell it?** **Thank you.**	

(Ask the following questions. Ask A first) **Where do you live / come from?** **Do you work or are you a student in ...?** **What do you do / study?** **Thank you.** **(Repeat for B)**	**Do you live in ...?** **Have you got a job?** **What job do you do? / What subject(s) do you study?**

Now answer these Phase 2 questions, paying attention to the verb tense you use. Remember to extend your answers (see Exam Information and Advice, page 29).

- *What will you do this evening?*
- *What is your favourite sport?*
- *How often do you watch television?*
- *Do you like going shopping? Why (not)?*
- *How did you celebrate your last birthday?*
- *What other language would you like to learn? Why?*

To finish Part One of the test, the examiner will say:

In the next part, you are going to talk to each other.

PART TWO (2–3 minutes)

In this part of the test the examiner will describe a situation and ask you to talk about it with your partner. You will be given a sheet with pictures to help you in your discussion. You will have to talk for about three minutes. The examiner will not take part in the discussion.

This is what the examiner says:

> **I am going to describe a situation to you.**
>
> **A seaside hotel has a large area to build a new facility for guests. Talk together about the facilities the hotel could build, and then decide which would be best for the guests.**
>
> **Here is a picture with some ideas to help you.**

You may want to use some of these ideas:

1   Do people need a swimming pool if they can swim in the sea? Guests who can't swim may be afraid of the sea? Use pool when the weather is bad?

2   Opinions of younger/older guests. Used every day? Noisy? Other discos in town?

3   Good to have a quiet area? People don't spend much time at the hotel? Lots of other things to do at the seaside? People bring their own books to read? Better to read out of doors?

4   Guests often want to check their emails? Other internet cafés in town? Play computer games?

5   Guests may want to keep fit or lose weight (they eat more on holiday)? On holiday you can have lots of exercise outside (swimming, walking)? Is it better to be in the open air and get a suntan?

PART THREE (3 minutes)

In Part Three, you will get a colour photograph to describe. You have to talk for about a minute and give a simple description of what you can see in the photograph. Your partner will get a different photograph on the same theme.

This is what the examiner (interlocutor) will say to you:

> **Now I'd like each of you to talk on your own about something. I am going to give each of you a photograph of people on holiday.**
>
> **Candidate A, here's your photograph. Please show it to Candidate B, but I'd like you to talk about it. Candidate B, you just listen, I'll give you your photograph in a moment.**
>
> **Candidate A, please tell us what you can see in your photograph.**

- *Turn to page 124 and talk about the photograph.*

> **Now, Candidate B, here is your photograph. It also shows people on holiday. Please show it to Candidate A and tell us what you can see in the photograph.**

- *Turn to page 125 and talk about the photograph.*

These are useful expressions you could use:

> In this picture, I can see …
>
> There's a (man) who is …
>
> Next to him there's a …
>
> I think they are enjoying (their holiday) because …
>
> I think it would be nice to go to this place because …

You may want to use some of this vocabulary:

Photo 1	Photo 2
tent/walking boots/rucksack/towel/boat	umbrellas
sleeping bag/thermos	sandy beach
by/close to the river	near the road
under a tree	rock mountains
having a chat/talking	(looks like a) castle
has taken off her boots/is wearing socks	swimming/walking/sunbathing
sitting/lying inside the tent	in the sun/in the shade
smiling/laughing/looking at each other	wearing sun hats
	must be hot
	clouds in the sky

Before doing this part of the test, read the Exam Information and Advice on the next page.

EXAM INFORMATION AND ADVICE

In Part Three you have to talk for about one minute about a photograph.

Talk about the people you can see:

- how many

- what they are doing (talking, relaxing)

- where they are (on holiday, in the country)

- what they are wearing (a shirt, shorts)

- describe their appearance (tall, young)

- say what you think: they may be married/she seems relaxed/perhaps he is thirsty/they look happy/he is probably English, etc.

Mention the things you can see:

- what they are

- size

- colour

- where they are.

You may not know, or may not remember, the names of some objects in the photograph. Do not worry about it. The examiners will give you credit if you try to explain what they are in your own words. For example, if you don't know the word 'frying pan', you could say: 'This is something you use to make chips, you put oil in it and fry potatoes'.

A DETAILED STUDY

These are descriptions of objects in the photograph on page 124 in a student's own words. Write the word for each of them.

1 Oh, I can't remember the word for this, in the middle of the photo. You stay in it when you go camping. This one's not very big, may be for one or two people. ....

2 I don't know the name for this. It's a kind of bag that you can carry on your back when you go for walks. You can carry everything you need in it. ....

3 Inside the tent there's a bag which is like a bed. You can sleep inside it and it keeps you really warm. ....

4 The boy's got a kind of bottle in his hands. You can keep a drink hot or cold in it. Maybe there's hot coffee in it. ....

5 On the tent there is a ... I can't remember the word ... you use it to dry yourself after a shower or after a swim in the river. ....

6 There's a pair of shoes here. They're special strong shoes for walking or climbing. ....

PART FOUR (3 minutes)

In Part Four, you and your partner speak together. The examiner (interlocutor) will tell you what you should talk about, and this is always connected with the theme of your photographs in Part Three. This is an opportunity to discuss your experiences, opinions, likes or dislikes with your partner. The examiner will not take part in the discussion.

This is what the examiner will say to you:

> **Your photographs showed people on holiday. Now, I'd like you to talk together about the kinds of holidays you enjoy and the kinds of holidays you would not enjoy.**

After approximately three minutes, the examiner will say:

> **Thank you, that's the end of the test.**

Here are some types of holiday to help you:

Holidays	
holidays with friends	group holidays
holidays with family	short holidays
mountain holidays	summer/winter holidays
camping holidays	walking holidays
holidays abroad	adventure holidays
holidays in a city	beach holidays

You may like to use some of these ideas to give reasons:

Reasons	
can/cannot rest	(don't) like climbing
(don't) get on with them	love visiting other countries
(no) time to relax	swimming is my favourite sport
(don't) have the same interests	do/don't speak the language
prefer/do not like hot weather	like to have evening activities
can/can't ski	lots of noise/too quiet
too dangerous	

Part 3: Mark the number of the question you are answering here ↑ Q7 or Q8

Write your answer below.

Do not write below this line

This section for use by SECOND Examiner only

Mark:

| 0 | 1.1 | 1.2 | 1.3 | 2.1 | 2.2 | 2.3 | 3.1 | 3.2 | 3.3 | 4.1 | 4.2 | 4.3 | 5.1 | 5.2 | 5.3 |

Examiner Number:

0	1	2	3	4	5	6	7	8	9
0	1	2	3	4	5	6	7	8	9
0	1	2	3	4	5	6	7	8	9

For **Writing (Parts 1 and 2):**

Write your answers clearly in the spaces provided.

Part 1: Write your answers below.

Do not write here

1	1	0
2	1	2	0
3	1	3	0
4	1	4	0
5	1	5	0

Part 2 (Question 6): Write your answer below.

Put your answer to Writing Part 3 on **Answer Sheet 2** ↑

Do not write below (Examiner use only)

| 0 | 1 | 2 | 3 | 4 | 5 |

TEST FOUR

PAPER 1: READING   1 hour

PART ONE

Questions 1–5

- Look at the text in each question.
- What does it say?
- Mark the correct letter (**A**, **B** or **C**).

- *In the exam you will mark your answers on a separate answer sheet (see page 33).*

Example:

0

A   There will be delays on night trains tomorrow.

B   There will be two night trains every hour tomorrow.

C   There will be more night trains from platform 6 tomorrow.

Answer:

1

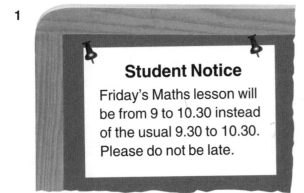

A   Friday's Maths lesson will be shorter than usual.

B   Friday's Maths lesson will finish later than usual.

C   Friday's Maths lesson will start earlier than usual.

2

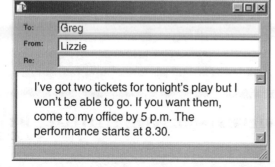

What is Lizzie doing?

A   inviting Greg to go to the theatre with her

B   offering Greg theatre tickets she has got

C   apologizing to Greg for not going to the theatre

3

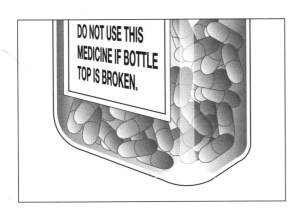

DO NOT USE THIS MEDICINE IF BOTTLE TOP IS BROKEN.

A   You must be careful not to break the bottle top when opening it.

B   You should only use this medicine if the bottle top is unbroken.

C   You have to use this medicine as soon as you break the bottle top.

4

Adriana
We've got nothing for dinner.
I'm going out to get us some
steak. Can you boil a few
potatoes?
I'll be back at 8.30.
                George

A   George wants to have dinner with Adriana when he returns.

B   George will have dinner out before returning at 8.30.

C   George is asking Adriana to have her dinner before he returns.

5

To	Mario
From	Luis
Time	11.10 a.m.
Re	Library book

Mario
Gus phoned from the library. They've got the book you asked them for. Get it today or they'll lend it to someone else.
        Luis

What must Mario do today?

A   Return a book to the library.

B   Collect a book from the library.

C   Phone the library about a book.

PART TWO

Questions 6–10

- The people below all want to find a place to stay.
- On the opposite page there are descriptions of places to stay.
- Decide which holiday accommodation would be the most suitable for the following people.
- For questions **6–10**, mark the correct letter (**A–H**).

- *In the exam you will mark your answers on a separate answer sheet (on page 33).*

6

Dina and Sam want to stay in the countryside with all meals included. They don't drive, so they need to be near train or bus services. They want to go horse-riding and see some wildlife.

7

Yuki wants to stay no more than a fifteen minute walk from the city's main attractions. She wants to be able to have dinner in different places every evening and go to concerts and plays.

8

Micky and David want a quiet place where they can ride horses and then go into the city centre for a drink. They don't have much money, so they want to cook their own meals.

9

Sebastian wants to stay in or near the hills. He wants to climb some of the highest hills but needs an experienced walker to accompany him. He needs to use email to contact his family.

10

Tom and Sheila want to stay in a quiet place with a car park and be able to drive to the city centre in under fifteen minutes. They want dinner at the hotel and a swimming pool for their children.

The Best Hotels, Hostels and Guesthouses
Find your ideal place to stay ...

A   **Clarendon House** is a family hotel in a peaceful location 10 km from the city centre, but with a good 24-hour bus service. Although only breakfast is provided, there is a fully-equipped kitchen for guests to use. Horses are available for hire and there is a large swimming pool very near the hotel.

B   **The Mountain Hostel** is in the middle of very high hills and can be reached only by car. Without telephones, computers or television, this is an ideal place to relax. All meals can be provided, but the hotel also has a kitchen for guests to cook if they wish to. There are daily guided walks to see the local wildlife.

C   **Jeremy's Guesthouse** is in a beautiful valley in the hills. Riding, tennis and golf are all available locally and the owner, an expert in mountain climbing, organizes walks. The nearest village is 10 km away, but the guesthouse offers everything you may need, including all food, theatre performances by a local group and free access to internet services.

D   **The Greenway Hotel** is a twenty-minute drive from the motorway and only ten minutes on foot from the city's theatre area. Meals are not provided (except breakfast), but there are several good quality restaurants nearby. Internet and email services are always available. The rooms are comfortable and very affordable. There is a large car park for guests.

E   **The Castle Hotel** is a half-hour drive from the city centre and very close to the railway station and motorway. Breakfast and lunch are provided and there is a good restaurant 20 metres from the hotel. The hotel offers evening concerts by local musicians and has wide-screen television and Internet services.

F   **The Four Seasons Hotel** is in the hills but within walking distance of the railway station. It has a restaurant which serves breakfast, lunch and dinner, all cooked with the best local produce. The area is good for fishing and riding and the hotel organizes tours to see birds and rare plants.

G   **The Farley Guesthouse** is on the seafront and all rooms have a view of either the beach or the hills behind the hotel. A number of sports are available, including surfing and tennis. Breakfast and lunch can be provided on request. There is a good restaurant, a cinema and an internet café nearby.

H   **The Sunrise Hotel** is only a ten-minute drive from the city centre but away from the traffic and noise. It has a swimming pool, a gym and a large garden. Breakfast and dinner can be served on request, and there is a café nearby which serves lunch. There is parking space behind the hotel.

PART THREE
Questions 11–20

- Look at the sentences below about women inventors.
- Read the text on the opposite page to decide if each sentence is correct or incorrect.
- If it is correct, mark **A**.
- If it is not correct, mark **B**.

- *In the exam you will mark your answers on a separate answer sheet (see page 33).*

---

11 There were a large number of women inventors in the 19th and early 20th centuries.

12 When Margaret Knight was twelve, she told her parents she wanted to work in a factory.

13 Margaret Knight's first invention made a machine stop when it became dangerous to use.

14 Margaret Knight won her fight to be considered the inventor of a machine to make paper bags.

15 In the 19th century, being an inventor was as difficult for a woman as being a business person.

16 Margaret Knight always had great difficulty finding a buyer for her inventions.

17 Women found that the covers of Beulah Henry's parasol often came off in the wind.

18 Beulah Henry was encouraged to invent her parasol by large umbrella manufacturers.

19 There is plenty of information about Beulah Henry's private life.

20 Beulah Henry was prepared to admit that her technical skills were not very developed.

Two Great Women Inventors

In the 19th and early 20th centuries, women had limited opportunities for a technical education and career, and few of them had an independent income. However, the history of women inventors in this period is very long. What sorts of women chose to become inventors under such difficult circumstances? The personal stories of two of them will give you an idea.

The nineteenth-century inventor Margaret Knight was born in the USA in 1838. As a young girl, she was made to work in a cotton factory by her parents. While she was working there, there was an accident and somebody was almost killed by a machine. Margaret was only 12 at the time, but she invented a way to fix the machine so that if there was the same fault again, straight away the machine would shut down completely.

She had more than eighty inventions, from a machine for cutting shoes to improvements for the steam engine. But her most important invention – a machine that produced paper bags with flat bottoms – never made her much money. In fact, the idea for the original invention was stolen by the person who made the model for the machine. She had to go through a long legal battle to be finally recognized as the owner of the idea.

In those days, women were not encouraged to be business people any more than they were encouraged to be inventors. Once Margaret Knight had produced an invention, she would usually sell it to somebody for not much cash, and when she died in 1914, all she left was 275 dollars.

These women's lives and achievements will always inspire future generations of inventors.

Beulah Henry also began inventing things when she was a young girl. In 1912, at age 25, she got her first patent for an ice-cream freezer. A year later, she patented a parasol – an umbrella for the sun – with changeable covers so that a woman could match her parasol with her clothes. Working out how to fix the covers so that they would not fly away on windy days was difficult, but she managed to do it. In fact, as she herself put it, 'The biggest umbrella men in the country told me it could not be done.' The invention earned her about 50,000 dollars from the manufacturers.

In all, she patented 49 inventions. But for someone with such a long career, surprisingly little is known about Beulah Henry's personal life. She was born in the USA in 1887 and grew up in an artistic family. She entered university in 1909 and we suppose her education did not include technical or mechanical subjects, as she was always honest about her lack of such skills.

PART FOUR

Questions 21–25

- Read the text and questions below.
- For each question, mark the correct letter (**A**, **B**, **C** or **D**).

- *In the exam you will mark your answers on a separate sheet (see page 33).*

The Australian Outback Post Plane

Today I am accompanying Rowan Dougall, a postman in Queensland in the far north of Australia, on his daily delivery trip. Every day, Rowan Dougall sets off with his post bags in the tail of his little plane – not much bigger than a large family car – and flies across one of the wildest places on earth, Australia's Cape North, to reach the very remote inland areas called The Outback.

We fly just three hundred metres above dangerous crocodiles and snakes. This is one of the longest and most expensive postman trips in the world. However, a 50-cent stamp not only gets a letter posted to a neighbouring town, it will get it hand-delivered by flying postman to the furthest areas of the outback. To help with the cost, the plane takes three or four paying local people or tourists, and I am one of them.

In the back of the plane, there is a pile of post – envelopes of all sizes, newspapers, and a few parcels. Somehow I expected this post to look special, maybe to include some hats or cowboy boots, but this looks no more exciting than the post delivered to me in England. I look at some of the names and addresses, wondering about the people who are waiting for these letters and parcels.

Rowan's route is 2,000 km long, with 15 stops, and I get a chance to meet Sandy, who has just received an order of clothes from a store. 'I look forward to this weekly delivery … there's not much that you can't get delivered out here,' she says, 'but I do miss actually going shopping.' Rowan is checking the time. There are another ten stops to make before dusk. Time to leap back on the plane and up into the air.

---

21   What is the writer's main purpose in writing the text?

   A   to get more support for postal services in the outback

   B   to show the wild beauty of the Australian outback

   C   to describe postal delivery services in the outback

   D   to warn about the dangers to postmen in the outback

22   What does the writer say about the expense of delivering mail to Cape North?

   A   Passenger fares help to cover some of the expense.

   B   People in the outback pay 50 cents for a delivery.

   C   It may be possible to find a less expensive system.

   D   The sender pays more than the usual postage.

23 What surprises the writer about the items of post on the plane?

    A   Some of the items are very unusual.

    B   The items are similar to his own post.

    C   He can see no clear names on the items.

    D   The items seem to be disorganized.

24 When talking about the plane post service, Sandy says that

    A   there are many items that cannot be delivered to her.

    B   she would like the service to be more frequent.

    C   the mail plane does not stop long enough there.

    D   she would like to be able to do her own shopping.

25 What might the writer say to a friend when he gets back?

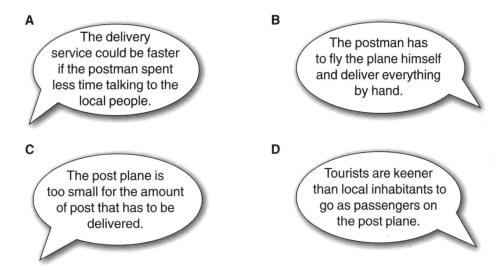

A The delivery service could be faster if the postman spent less time talking to the local people.

B The postman has to fly the plane himself and deliver everything by hand.

C The post plane is too small for the amount of post that has to be delivered.

D Tourists are keener than local inhabitants to go as passengers on the post plane.

Before doing this part of the test, read the Exam Information and Advice on the next page.

EXAM INFORMATION AND ADVICE

In Part Four, there is a text of about 300 words followed by five multiple-choice questions with four options, A, B, C and D. The text includes attitudes and opinions as well as facts.

1   Read the questions and the text once fairly quickly to get an idea of the topic and general meaning of the text.

2   Think about the writer's purpose.

3   Read the text again very carefully and then start dealing with the questions one by one, checking your answer each time with the text.

4   The first question always tests writer purpose. To find the answer, you need to read the whole text. So, if you are not sure of the answer, leave this question to the end. Learn the meaning of words that describe writer purpose, e.g. *advise, complain, describe, encourage, explain, inform, insist, suggest* and *warn*.

5   Questions 22, 23 and 24 may test opinion, attitude and/or detail. They follow the order of information in the text.

6   Question 25 tests global understanding and the four options are longer. You will need to look back at different parts of the text to answer this question.

A DETAILED STUDY

Look at the short texts below (1–3) and match each one with a writer purpose (a, b or c).

1   *We need to be careful to avoid the problems we had in the past. This time they might be more serious.*

    a)   to complain about present problems

    b)   to explain the reasons for past problems

    c)   to warn about possible future problems

2   *The hotel is in one of the most beautiful parts of the city and so it should do better than it actually does. All the managers would need to do is provide certain facilities for guests.*

    a)   to describe the area where the hotel is

    b)   to suggest improvements to the hotel

    c)   to encourage people to stay at the hotel

3   *I am going to say this just once, and I hope you will all take notice of my words. You are now in your final year at school and you need some experience of the real world before you go to university. There is no better way to do this than by taking a year out and travelling.*

    a)   to encourage students to travel

    b)   to inform students about school travel

    c)   to advise students on places to travel to

PART FIVE

Questions 26–35

- Read the text below and choose the correct word for each space.
- For each question, mark the correct letter (**A**, **B**, **C** or **D**).

- *In the exam you will mark your answers on a separate answer sheet (see page 33).*

Example:

0   **A**   retired   **B**   left   **C**   gone   **D**   moved

Answer: | 0 | A | B | C | D |

FROM SCHOOLBOY TO CLOWN

Gareth Ellis is the youngest of Alan and Kath's sons. His two older brothers have already

(0) ………..…….. their parents' home. **(26)** ………….….... he is only twelve, Gareth is sure that he will

be a clown. When Gareth was three, his parents **(27)** …………….... him to see Zippo's circus and he

(28) ……….…....... remembers that visit today. All Gareth **(29)** ....……….…... for as birthday presents

was to go back to Zippo's, his father **(30)** .....………….… .

Then, in 1996, Alan **(31)** ...…………... his job, so, together with Kath, they decided to try and find full-

time jobs in a circus **(32)** …………....... Gareth would have a chance to learn clown skills. **(33)** …………......

of them got jobs with the Moscow State Circus. Alan **(34)** ....………….. a lights operator and Kath was

in the box office. After two years there, the director of Zippo's offered them jobs and training for Gareth.

One day Gareth **(35)** .....…………. to be the best clown in the world.

26	**A**	However	**B**	Although	**C**	Even	**D**	So
27	**A**	went	**B**	travelled	**C**	carried	**D**	took
28	**A**	since	**B**	already	**C**	still	**D**	yet
29	**A**	demanded	**B**	requested	**C**	asked	**D**	wanted
30	**A**	says	**B**	speaks	**C**	informs	**D**	tells
31	**A**	missed	**B**	lost	**C**	gave	**D**	threw
32	**A**	when	**B**	where	**C**	which	**D**	who
33	**A**	Any	**B**	Some	**C**	Either	**D**	Both
34	**A**	became	**B**	turned	**C**	worked	**D**	applied
35	**A**	believes	**B**	hopes	**C**	thinks	**D**	dreams

Before doing this part of the test, read the Exam Information and Advice on the next page.

EXAM INFORMATION AND ADVICE

In Part Five, you read a short text with ten gaps and an example. After the text, there are ten multiple-choice questions with four options for each gap. This part tests mainly vocabulary, but also some grammatical points.

1 Before answering any questions, read through the text to understand the topic and the general meaning.

2 Go back to the beginning of the text and study the example.

3 Start with the first gap. Read the complete sentence to make sure you choose the correct option. Think whether the word you have chosen fits grammatically, i.e. does it go well with the words that follow? Try the other three options in the gap to make sure that they do not fit.

4 When you have completed all the answers, read the whole text again to check that it makes sense.

5 Transfer your answers carefully on to Answer Sheet 1, Part Five (see page 33).

A DETAILED STUDY

Read the following sentences and study the way the words in italics are used. Decide which words in italics would best fit the gaps in the text on page 99.

26	*However*	I am very busy. *However*, I will find time to help you.
	Although	*Although* I am very busy, I'll find time to help you.
	Even	*Even* though I am very busy, I'll find time to help you.
	so	I am very busy, *so* I won't be able to help you.

27	*went*	Alice *went* with her students to see a concert in the city.
	travelled	Alice *travelled* with her students to see a concert in the city.
	carried	Alice *carried* her trumpet to the concert.
	took	Alice *took* her students to see a concert in the city.

28	*since*	Mark had been a good swimmer *since* he was a child.
	already	It was only nine o'clock and Mark had *already* had a swim.
	still	Mark is eighty years old, but he *still* swims every day.
	yet	Mark is eighty, but he hasn't given up swimming *yet*.

29	*demanded*	They *demanded* more information about the accident.
	requested	They *requested* more information about the accident.
	asked	They *asked* for more information about the accident.
	wanted	They *wanted* more information about the accident.

30	*says*	My father often *says* that he dislikes modern music.
	speaks	My father often *speaks* about his dislike for modern music.
	informs	My father often *informs* people that he dislikes modern music.
	tells	My father often *tells* people that he dislikes modern music.

31	*missed*	Alice liked her new job, but she *missed* her former colleagues.
	lost	Alice had a teaching job, but unfortunately she *lost* it last year.
	gave	Alice was working full-time, so she *gave* up her French studies.
	threw	Alice *threw* away all her old books and bought new ones.

32 *when*   Paula opened her shop at a time *when* it was really needed.
where   Paula had a shop *where* you could buy all kinds of food.
which   Paula opened a food shop *which* sold all kinds of food.
who   Paula had a shop assistant *who* helped her every day.

33 *any*   Bert has five cousins, but have *any* of them ever visited him?
some   Bert invited his friends to a party but only *some* of them came.
either   Ask Jon or Bert. *Either* of them would know the answer.
both   Jon and Bert liked music. *Both* of them came to the concert.

34 *became*   Cindy studied hard and *became* a very good doctor.
turned   Cindy has *turned* into a beautiful woman.
worked   Cindy *worked* as a doctor in a small town.
applied   Cindy *applied* for a job as a doctor in a small town.

35 *believes*   Nigel *believes* that he will win the race on Sunday.
hopes   Nigel *hopes* to win the race on Sunday.
thinks   Nigel *thinks* (that) he will win the race on Sunday.
dreams   Nigel *dreams* of winning the race on Sunday.

For the answers, see the key to Test Four, Reading Part 5 on page 144.

PAPER 1: WRITING 30 minutes

PART ONE

Questions 1–5

- Here are some sentences about a castle.
- For each question, complete the second sentence so that it means the same as the first.
- **Use no more than three words.**
- Write only the missing words.

- *In the exam you will write your answers on a separate answer sheet (see page 89).*

Example:

0　Old Farham Castle <u>was bu</u>ilt six hundred years <u>ago</u>.

　　Old Farham Castle .... **six hundred years old.**

Answer:　| **0** | *is* |

1　People say there is no other castle as interesting as this one in Europe.

　　People say that this is .... **castle in Europe.**

2　The castle opened to the public last year.

　　The castle .... **open to the public since last year.**

3　Students are allowed to visit the castle without paying anything.

　　Students .... **have to pay anything to visit the castle.**

4　Visitors are always met at the door by the owner, Mr Brandon.

　　The owner, Mr Brandon, always .... **visitors at the door.**

5　I asked Mr Brandon if he lived in the castle when he was a child.

　　I asked Mr Brandon: '.. **live in the castle when you were a child?'**

PART TWO
Question 6

You have joined a new sports club.

Write an email to your English friend, Phil. In your email, you should:

- say where the club is

- explain why you like it

- invite Phil to join it too.

Write **35–45 words.**

- *In the exam you will write your answer on a separate answer sheet (see page 89).*

PART THREE

Questions 7–8

Write an answer to **one** of the questions (**7** or **8**).

Write about **100 words** on your answer sheet.

Question 7

- This is part of a letter you receive from an English friend.

> *I'm thinking of buying a mobile phone. Do you think it's a good idea? Do people in your country use mobile phones a lot?*

- Now write a letter, answering your friend's questions.
- Write your **letter** in about 100 words.

- *In the exam you will write your answer on a separate answer sheet (see page 89).*

Question 8

- You want to write a story for a competition in a magazine.
- This is the title for your story:

  ### *The lost suitcase*

- Write your **story** in about 100 words.

- *In the exam you will write your answer on a separate answer sheet (see page 89).*

Before doing question 8, read the Exam Information and Advice on the next page.

EXAM INFORMATION AND ADVICE

In Part Three, you have a choice of task: either an informal letter or a story of about 100 words.

The story

The question will give you a short title or the first sentence of the story. Your story must have a beginning, a development (the body of the story) and an end.

A story is usually in the past tense, so you need to revise all the past forms of verbs. Try to write at least 90 words and don't worry if your answer is a bit longer than 100 words. Your answer should not be under 80 words.

In this part, you will get better marks if you use different tenses, vocabulary and expressions. Use the language you know and don't be afraid of making mistakes. When you have finished, check your spelling and grammar.

1   Read the title or the first sentence carefully.

2   Before you start writing, think of how the story is going to develop. Think of a simple plan for your story and write down a few words. For example:

       • What happened at the beginning? (was travelling by train, my suitcase disappeared)

       • What happened after that? (went to the police)

       • How did it end? (I found it/it was empty)

3   Start writing and include all the details as you write, e.g. where you were travelling, who you were with, colour/size/contents of suitcase, what the police told you to do, etc.

4   Make sure your story is easy to read. Use words such as *Then …, After that, … While …, When …, In the morning, …*

5   Read your story and check the language. Have you used different verb tenses? Are your verbs in the correct tense? Have you used some adjectives, e.g. *heavy, large, interesting*, and adverbs, e.g. *quickly, carefully*?

A DETAILED STUDY

1 Link the sentences A and B to make one sentence using all of the linking expressions below. Remember to link sentences in your story.

    A *Carlos saw that the suitcase was empty.*   **B** *He went to the police.*

    a) when

    b) so

    c) as soon as …

    d) because

    A *Carlos looked everywhere for his suitcase.*   **B** *He couldn't find it.*

    e) but

    f) (al)though

2 Read this sample answer. The writer has used the present instead of the past forms of verbs and he has not given an ending to the story.

    a) Correct the verbs which are in the wrong tense (present instead of past).

    b) Add an ending to the story.

The lost suitcase

Last night <u>is</u> a beautiful night. <u>I'm having</u> dinner with my friends in a restaurant. Suddenly we <u>hear</u> a big shout: 'Hey!' We all <u>look</u> at Paul. Paul shouted loudly 'I've lost my suitcase!' Then he <u>run</u> out of the restaurant. But Alan <u>stops</u> him. Alan <u>say</u> to Paul 'Keep calm, now you need to think carefully where you've been today.' After Paul <u>tell</u> us, we <u>go</u> everywhere that he had been – library, café, bus stop, cinema …

PAPER 2: LISTENING

PART ONE

Questions 1–7

- There are seven questions in this part.
- For each question there are three pictures and a short recording.
- Choose the correct picture and put a tick (✔) in the box below it.

- *In the exam you will write your answers on the question paper and then you will have six minutes to copy them on to the answer sheet (see page 119).*

Example: Which musical instrument will the man buy?

A

B ☐

C ☐

---

1 What did the man dislike about the party?

A ☐

B ☐

C ☐

2 For which concert should you book tickets in advance?

A ☐

B ☐

C ☐

3   What will they buy for their friend Jill?

A ☐   B ☐   C ☐

4   What will the weather be like in the hills tomorrow?

A ☐   B ☐   C ☐

5   Where is the present now?

A ☐   B ☐   C ☐

6 Which job will the girl apply for?

A ☐   B ☐   C ☐

7 At what time is the *World Music* radio programme today?

A ☐   B ☐   C ☐

PART TWO
Questions 8–13

- You will hear a radio interview with Philip Samson, a famous mountain bike racer.
- For each question, put a tick (✔) in the correct box.

- *In the exam you will write your answers on the question paper and then you will have six minutes to copy them on to the answer sheet (see page 119).*

8	Why did Philip start riding mountain bikes?	A	He was tired of doing other sports.	☐
		B	He was keen to enter a competition.	☐
		C	He was sure he had the skills for it.	☐
9	Before Philip took part in the World Cup, his mother	A	suggested he spent more time training.	☐
		B	said he had no chances of winning.	☐
		C	encouraged his fans to go and support him.	☐
10	What does Philip like to do as soon as he finishes a race?	A	give TV interviews	☐
		B	chat with his fans	☐
		C	sign autographs	☐
11	Philip says that, compared to other racers, he	A	works harder in the gym.	☐
		B	trains on more difficult roads.	☐
		C	has the best bike available.	☐
12	What does Philip say about mountain bike magazines?	A	They have few articles about competitions.	☐
		B	They sell more copies than they used to.	☐
		C	They are mostly read by professional racers.	☐
13	As well as racing, what is Philip planning to do?	A	appear in a film	☐
		B	publish a book	☐
		C	advertise bikes	☐

PART THREE

Questions 14–19

- You will hear a travel agent talking on the radio about a holiday in Sri Lanka.
- For each question, fill in the missing information in the numbered space.

- *In the exam you will write your answers on the question paper and then you will have six minutes to copy them on to the answer sheet (see page 119).*

A Holiday in Sri Lanka

Visitors come to the west coast of Sri Lanka for the

(14) .... as well as the walks and bird life.

In the hotel gardens there are more than **(15)** .... types of

tree.

Every hotel room has a **(16)** .... on the ceiling.

On one of the organized tours, visitors can learn how

(17) .... are made.

There will be a visit to a country house where visitors can meet the

(18) .... and see works of art.

The holiday price does <u>not</u> include either the **(19)** .... or

the travel insurance.

PART FOUR

Questions 20–25

- Look at the six sentences for this part.
- You will hear a young woman, Carol, and a young man, David, talking about their plans for the weekend.
- Decide if each sentence is correct or incorrect.
- If it is correct, put a tick (✔) in the box under **A** for **YES**. If it is not correct, put a tick (✔) in the box under **B** for **NO**.

- *In the exam you will write your answers on the question paper and then you will have six minutes to copy them on to the answer sheet (see page 119).*

		A YES	B NO
20	Carol is looking forward to visiting her aunt on Saturday.	☐	☐
21	David has some work to finish this weekend.	☐	☐
22	David is confident that he can get tickets for a music show.	☐	☐
23	Carol and David decide to go and see a film on Saturday evening.	☐	☐
24	Carol thinks her weekends are less active than David's.	☐	☐
25	David persuades Carol to go surfing with him on Sunday.	☐	☐

Before doing this part of the test, read the Exam Information and Advice on the next page.

EXAM INFORMATION AND ADVICE

In Part Four you listen to an informal conversation in which two people express their attitudes and opinions on a topic. The speakers will sometimes agree and sometimes disagree with each other. As you listen, you look at six sentences which report the opinions of the speakers and decide whether they are true or false according to what you hear. You will need to understand the general meaning of the conversation and also the detailed meaning of what each speaker says.

Listen for the general meaning first and choose the best option for each question. When you listen a second time, pay attention to the more detailed meaning and check carefully that your answers are correct.

Remember:

a) You will not hear the same words that you have on the page – you will hear similar words and expressions. For example, if on the page it says *X is looking forward to the party*, in the recording you may hear *X really wants to go to the party* or *X can't wait to go to the party*.

b) Both speakers may say something about each question, so you must pay attention to how they interact with each other: Who mentions a point first? Does the other one agree or disagree? Listen for expressions of agreement or disagreement, for example, *I don't think so./That's what I think, too.*

A DETAILED STUDY

Listen to Part Four again and answer the following questions by putting a tick (✔) in the correct box, either true or false. This will give you extra practice and help you check your answers to questions 20–25.

		True	False
1	Carol says that she really wants to visit her aunt.	☐	☐
2	David says he is free this weekend but was not free last weekend.	☐	☐
3	Carol says that she always has to work at weekends.	☐	☐
4	Carol mentions the Novo Band first.	☐	☐
5	Carol asks David if he has already bought his ticket.	☐	☐
6	David realizes that it won't be easy to get tickets.	☐	☐
7	Carol has seen a good film recently.	☐	☐
8	David has already seen the same film.	☐	☐
9	David says he does not enjoy going to the cinema.	☐	☐
10	Carol says that she seldom practises sports at weekends.	☐	☐
11	Carol is at first unwilling to go surfing with David.	☐	☐
12	David says he is good at surfing.	☐	☐

Now check your answers to these questions and then decide if you want to change any of your Part Four answers on page 112.

PAPER 3: SPEAKING

PART ONE (2–3 minutes)

In Part One the examiner (interlocutor) will ask each of you some personal questions – your name, where you live, about your work or studies, about your free time activities, etc. The questions can be about the past, the present or the future.

Preliminary English Test
Speaking Test

Part 1 (2–3 minutes)

Phase 1
Interlocutor

**A/B   Good morning / afternoon / evening.
Can I have your mark sheets, please?**

**A/B   I'm .... and this is ....
He/she is just going to listen to us.**

**A   Now, what's your name?
Thank you.**

**B   And, what's your name?
Thank you.**

Back-up prompts

**B   What's your surname?
How do you spell it?**

Thank you.

**A   And, what's your surname?
How do you spell it?**

Thank you.

How do you write your family/second name?

(Ask the following questions. Ask A first)

Where do you live / come from?

**Do you work or are you a student in ...?
What do you do / study?**

Thank you.

(Repeat for B)

Do you live in ...?

**Have you got a job?
What job do you do? / What subject(s) do you study?**

Now answer these Phase 2 questions, paying attention to the verb tense you use. Remember to give full answers (see Exam Information and Advice, page 29).

- *What magazines do you like?*
- *What do you usually do at weekends?*
- *Do you like going to the cinema? Why (not)?*
- *What country would you like to visit? Why?*
- *What was your favourite food when you were a child?*
- *When did you start learning English?*

To finish Part One of the test, the examiner will say:

In the next part, you are going to talk to each other.

PART TWO (2–3 minutes)

In this part of the test the examiner will describe a situation and ask you to talk about it with your partner. You will be given a sheet with pictures to help you in your discussion. You will have to talk for about three minutes. The examiner will not take part in the discussion.

This is what the examiner says:

> **I am going to describe a situation to you.**
>
> **A college is going to offer students a special class on Saturday mornings. Talk together about the different classes they could offer, and decide which would be most interesting for the students.**
>
> **Here is a picture with some ideas to help you.**

You may want to use some of these words:

useful/interesting/healthy/necessary/fun/enjoyable/exciting/important/entertaining/relaxing

boring/tiring/uninteresting/hard work/unnecessary

PART THREE (3 minutes)

In Part Three, you will get a colour photograph to describe. You have to give a simple description of what you can see in the photograph and talk for about a minute. Your partner will get a different photograph on the same theme.

This is what the examiner (interlocutor) will say to you:

> **Now I'd like each of you to talk on your own about something. I am going to give each of you a photograph of people writing.**
>
> **Candidate A, here's your photograph. Please show it to Candidate B, but I'd like you to talk about it. Candidate B, you just listen, I'll give you your photograph in a moment.**
>
> **Candidate A, please tell us what you can see in your photograph.**

● *Turn to page 126 and talk about the photograph.*

> **Now, Candidate B, here's your photograph. It also shows people writing. Please show it to Candidate A and tell us what you can see in the photograph.**

● *Turn to page 127 and talk about the photograph.*

You may want to use some of this vocabulary and these expressions:

people of different ages	posters/animals
a woman in her fifties or sixties	toys
girls/daughters/son	enjoying the experience/working together
sitting/standing/holding baby	looking at each other
helping her daughters	learning
paying attention	blouse/jumper/shirt
man about forty years old	desk/papers/folders/books/notebooks
students/teachers/employees	white board
talking	two of them writing/have got pencils
laughing	they may be writing reports, homework, etc
smiling	holding a pencil in her right hand
bedroom	doing homework/computer
white bed, some pillows	school girl

PART FOUR (3 minutes)

In Part Four, you and your partner speak together. The examiner (interlocutor) will tell you what you should talk about, and this is always connected with the theme of your photographs in Part Three. This is an opportunity to discuss your experiences, opinions, likes or dislikes with your partner. The examiner will not take part in the discussion.

This is what the examiner will say to you:

> **Your photographs showed people writing. Now, I'd like you to talk together about the things you like to write for work or for school and the things you find difficult to write.**

After approximately three minutes, the examiner will say:

> **Thank you, that's the end of the test.**

Before doing this part of the test, read the Exam Information and Advice on the next page.

EXAM INFORMATION AND ADVICE

Read again what the examiner asks you to do in Part Four: *Now I'd like to talk together about ... and ... about ...* The examiner will always ask you to talk about two points. When you have said enough about the first point, talk about the second point. Don't be afraid to express opinions and say what you like and what you do not like. The examiner will not give you marks for your opinions but will listen to the language you use.

Keep talking with your partner until the examiner tells you it is enough. If you stop too soon, the examiner may ask you another question.

This is a conversation with your partner. Don't forget to ask for his/her comments and opinions:

- How about you?
- What do you think?
- Do you agree?

A DETAILED STUDY

From Column A, choose ideas that you could use for the first part of the question (what you like) and from Column B choose ideas you could use for the second part (what you find difficult to write).

Column A	Column B
I like/I don't like writing ...	**I find it difficult because ...**
letters to family	it takes a long time
letters to friends	I find it boring
emails	I can't write very well
stories	my spelling is not very good
poems	I prefer to phone people
homework	my handwriting is not clear
reports	I don't like to type
things in my language	I don't have enough vocabulary
things in a foreign language	
songs	

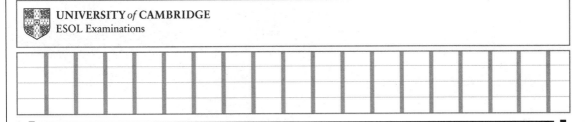

UNIVERSITY *of* **CAMBRIDGE**
ESOL Examinations

Candidate Name
If not already printed, write name
in CAPITALS and complete the
Candidate No. grid (in pencil).

Candidate Signature

SAMPLE

Examination Title

Centre

Centre No.

Candidate No.

Examination Details

Supervisor:
If the candidate is ABSENT or has WITHDRAWN shade here ⊏⊐

PET Paper 2 Listening Candidate Answer Sheet

You must transfer all your answers from the Listening Question Paper to this answer sheet.

Instructions

Use a PENCIL (B or HB).

Rub out any answer you want to change with an eraser.

For **Parts 1, 2** and **4:**
Mark ONE letter for each question.
For example, if you think **A** is the right answer to the
question, mark your answer sheet like this:

For **Part 3:**
Write your answers clearly in the spaces next
to the numbers (14 to 19) like this:

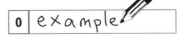

Part 1	Part 2	Part 3	Do not write here	Part 4
1 A B C	8 A B C	14	1 14 0	20 A B
2 A B C	9 A B C	15	1 15 0	21 A B
3 A B C	10 A B C	16	1 16 0	22 A B
4 A B C	11 A B C	17	1 17 0	23 A B
5 A B C	12 A B C	18	1 18 0	24 A B
6 A B C	13 A B C	19	1 19 0	25 A B
7 A B C				

DP493/391

KEY AND EXPLANATION

TEST ONE

p.6   READING   Part One

1   **B**: Sylvia says *Be home by then – I'll be out.*

2   **A**: the repair works go from Tuesday until Sunday (notice *can't be visited … until Monday*)

3   **C**: *Could you let me know the number of students?* shows Sandra needs details.

4   **B**: books *must be left* on tables

5   **C**: *out of reach of children* means somewhere where children cannot see / touch it.

FURTHER PRACTICE AND GUIDANCE (p.8)

A Detailed Study

1   **1 d**   The artwork helps you.
    2 a   The museum is a building.
    3 f   This is an email.
    4 b   About books / note from librarian
    5 e   The artwork helps you.

2   **1 c**   Notice *Be home from work by then.*
    2 b   Come back when the museum is open.
    3 d   *the number of students* = some details about the party
    4 a   Library users are told to leave books on the tables.
    5 f   a safe place to keep a bottle of medicine / dangerous chemicals

p.10   READING   Part Two

6   **G**: *a travel writer* (travelling and also writing), *willing to spend at least two weeks* a *month travelling* (does not mind spending long periods abroad), *starting immediately* (could start tomorrow)
D needs a reporter, but Carl has no experience of deep-sea photography.

7   **E**: *knowledge of animals* (a degree in zoology), *a real team player* (works well with other people), *at least one foreign language* (speaks German)
F is wrong, she is not keen on sports and the job requires swimming skills.

8   **C**: *to cover the summer months* (an exciting summer job), *give you training* (learn new skills), *excellent swimming skills* (trained as a deep-sea diver) *some experience of working with different age groups* (has taken groups of children and adults)
F is wrong because the job is longer and he does not speak any foreign languages. D is wrong as he has no experience of deep-sea photography.

9   **H**: *spend up to six months per year …* (several months abroad), *must have a driving licence* (used to take tourists in her own car), *basic knowledge of Spanish* (can hold a simple conversation)
B is wrong because no actual travelling is involved. F is wrong because it requires an excellent command of Spanish.

10   **B**: *Foreign travel is not in the job description* (does not require her to travel abroad), *must speak French or Spanish or German* (speaks Spanish), *we work on Saturdays in the summer months* (willing to work at weekends)
A, F and H are wrong as they all require travelling.

p.12   READING   Part Three

11   **B**: *the inhabitants of Jura are proud …* (of their quiet life)

12   **A**: *an early start is essential for a safe return …*

13   **A**: *From the moment you get off the ferry …*

14   **B**: *would do well to have … within easy reach.*

15   **B**: *an information board … and a box*, but no person there.

16   **B**: the walks divide when you are *over a small stream … here you turn left …*

17   **A**: *plants from far-away countries*

18   **B**: *what you would expect to pay in other parts …*

19   **B**: *selection of goods on offer … waterproofs and sleeping bags …*

20   **A**: *have the goods you need delivered … for your arrival*

p.14   READING   Part Four

21 C: He is answering the question *people often ask me who I have to thank for my success …*
A: He does not give advice about how children should learn.
B: He does not describe his job or his daily life as a musician.
D: He says nobody taught him to play but he does not complain about it (*I … had musical talent and that is all you need.*)

22 A: His parents allowed him to sit at the piano … *as long as he wanted.*
B: *they never mentioned it*
C: *didn't suggest I should take lessons*
D: *The songs just came to me when I had my hands on the piano.*

23 C: *the words were from other songwriters*
A: he copied *other people's best songs* (they were not badly written)
B: *It seemed so easy.*
D: he developed his own style later, when he was *beyond … teenage years*

24 B: … *make a living as a musician but I had my doubts*
A: His parents had developed *a strong belief* that he would become a musician.
C: He took the job after school, but he does not say what he learnt in school.
D: *that changed everything* refers to one of his songs winning a prize, not to the radio job

25 B: The writer believes all songwriters *copy other people's songs* to begin with.
A: His family did not guide him, they just let him play and develop his talent (*allowed me to sit at the piano*)
C: He started creating songs when he was a child, and then *proper* songs when he was a teenager. His early years were important.
D: He became successful without formal teaching, *talent … is all you need*

p.16   READING   Part Five

26 C: You *spend* (or *have*) a holiday; you *tour* a place; you *pass* the time; you stay *in* or *at* a place

27 B: *Said* does not need anything after it, the others do: *told* <u>me</u>, *talked* <u>about</u>, *spoke* <u>of</u>.

28 D: best *time* refers to a part of the day; *part* is incorrect without *of the day*; a *period* in history; I have an *hour* to get there

29 A: The writer knew he would have to wait, so he sat down.

30 C: *People* is a countable noun, so you say *many*, <u>not</u> *much* people; *all* (of) the other people or *lots of* people.

31 D: You *have* fun, you can't use *feel*, *get*, or *enjoy* with the word *fun*.

32 B: The writer thinks this is the ideal situation for dolphins – they *should* be free. *Ought*, *have* and *need* are followed by *to*: *ought to be, have to be, need to be*

33 C: *Found* goes with *out*; *looked out* means took care; *realized* and *learnt* are never followed by *out*.

34 A: the past participle of *be* is *been*. *Visited*, *come* and *gone* do not go with the preposition *in*.

35 A: *Return* is followed by the preposition *to* if we mention a place. But notice: return *on* 6 January, return *for* a holiday.

p.17   WRITING   Part One

1 It's a long time **since** I read a good novel.

2 If I were you, **I would/should** borrow a book from the library.

3 I think that novels are not **as interesting as** history books.

4 My local library has got only a **few** history books.

5 My brother isn't **old enough** to read computer books.

(Sometimes there is more than one way to complete the sentences correctly, for example, in 2, *would* and *should* are correct.)

FURTHER PRACTICE AND GUIDANCE (p.18)

A Detailed Study

1 **b:** *Since* is the word you need when the sentence starts with *It's a long time*, followed by a verb in the past.

2 **c:** You need *would borrow*, which is a conditional form after *If I were you*.
A is incorrect because you do not use *to* after *would*. B is incorrect because there is a spelling mistake: *borow*.

3 **a:** The comparative form *not as … as* means that novels are *less interesting*.
B is wrong because of the word *not* – *not less interesting* – which is unnecessary, and in C the word *very* is grammatically incorrect (you need *as*).

4 **b:** *few* is used with countable nouns, *a few books*.
A is incorrect, we say *a small number/a large number*. C is incorrect: I have *a few* books, *A few of* my books are in French.

5 **c:** *too young = not old enough*. In A the structure is incorrect and in B the meaning is completely different from that of the first sentence.

p.19   WRITING   Part Two

Question 6
Model Answer

> Hi Jack
> They are showing *Without Fear* at the Odeon tomorrow at 8. I really want to see it! Would you like to come with me? We could meet at 7.30 at the cinema café.
> Emile

The email covers the 3 points:
- you have said what film you want to see: *Without Fear*
- you have invited Jack to see it: *Would you like to come with me?*
- you have suggested a time and a place to meet: *7.30 at the cinema café*.

p.20   WRITING   Part Three

Question 7
Model answer

> *Dear John*
>
> *Many thanks for your letter. I know that you love reading novels. I don't like them because they are usually so long! I prefer to read magazines about sports like climbing or wind-surfing. I buy one or two magazines every week. As you know, I am crazy about sport.*
>
> *I also like to read short stories, so I often borrow detective and mystery stories from the library. I have just finished one called 'Late for Dinner', about a man who has a road accident and forgets his own name. It has a happy ending!*
>
> *I hope to see you soon and we can talk about the things we read.*
>
> *All the best*
>
> *X*

The letter answers your friend's questions and
- it is well organized: 1. you mention John's letter 2. you say what you prefer to read and why 3. you give information about something you have read recently.
- it shows a good range of tenses/grammar/linking words: *I know that/because/are usually/As you know/so/have just finished/who/has/forgets/enjoyed*
- it shows good use of vocabulary: *climbing/wind-surfing/detective/mystery/library/accident*
- it has good opening and closing sentences: *Many thanks for your letter/I hope to see you soon and we can talk about the things we read.*

Question 8
Model answer

> *Tom was watching TV at home when he heard a noise upstairs. He turned off the TV and was very quiet for a few seconds. Then he heard the noise again. At first he thought it could be the cat, but then he remembered that the cat was outside. He was very frightened, so his legs started to shake.*
>
> *He went upstairs very slowly. He suddenly saw a big shadow on the wall. This strange shadow had three legs! He thought there was a monster in the bedroom. He walked slowly into the room and he saw his grandfather. He was dancing, using his walking-stick and a walkman! Tom laughed and was very happy that there was no monster!*

This is good story and
- it is well organized: 1. what Tom did first (turned off TV, was quiet) 2. how he felt (frightened) 3. what he did then (went upstairs) 4. what he saw and how it ended
- it shows a good range of tenses/grammar/ linking words: *turned off/At first he thought/could be/but/so/walked/saw/there was*
- it shows good use of vocabulary: *walking-stick/walkman/remembered/frightened/shadow/ grandfather/laughed*
- it has a good closing sentence: *Tom laughed and was very happy that there was no monster!*

p.21 LISTENING Part One

1 A: She says it will be too warm for a long-sleeved blouse.
B: Trousers are comfortable, but won't look as nice as a dress.
C: *A dress may not be as comfortable as trousers, but it'll look nicer. OK, when do you want to get it?*

2 A: Charles will walk through the park, but they won't meet there.
B: *but let's meet there anyway*
C: Charles says waiting in the café is better than waiting in the street.

3 **A:** *the lecture is now going to be on the 21st*
B: the 23rd was changed because Professor Brown has a meeting that day.
C: the 31st was suggested, but the room was not free.

4 **A:** *one video wasn't enough … so I also got a couple of novels*
B: *I seldom borrow CDs.*
C: He wanted to borrow 2 videos, but they only allow you to take one out.

5 A: The information in the newspaper will come tomorrow.
B: *that's how I learnt about it, in the ten o'clock sports news*
C: The man will phone the woman when he has more details

6 A: They missed the wildlife programme because they didn't know about it.
B: They saw the thriller months ago, and they may watch it again tonight.
C: *while we had Channel 4 on for the news*

7 **A:** *you won't be able to do this (mountain climbing) by yourselves*
B: *… and you can do it on your own.*
C: *you'll be accompanied by one of our guides*

FURTHER PRACTICE AND GUIDANCE (p.24)

A Detailed Study
1 1 d
   2 f
   3 b
   4 g
   5 a
   6 e
   7 c

2 a) 1, 3, 4, 5, 6
   b) 7
   c) 2

p.25 LISTENING Part Two

8 A: Her friend became an actress, it was not the job Clara wanted.
B: *I was dreaming of being a teacher.*
C: Most of Clara's schoolmates wanted to be lawyers, but Clara didn't.

9 A: Clara's mother was upset because Clara was taking a long time to decide.
B: Clara does not say the job seemed very difficult.
C: *I was afraid it wouldn't be interesting working on my own … with no-one to talk to.*

10 **A:** *… there were some big boxes full of museum objects for me downstairs … Could I go and get them?*
B: Her colleague said a few words, not Clara.
C: She met her colleagues, but she does not say that was a surprise.

11 A: No. She had enough knowledge of computers.
B: No. She had to give up her French studies.
C: *For that you need an understanding of basic mathematics. My boss said I definitely should do something about it, and I did.*

12 A: Preparing exhibitions is less exciting than research work.
B: *writing short histories of museum objects … I find this research work much more exciting than preparing an important exhibition.*
C: Clara doesn't get many opportunities to talk to visitors.

13 A: Clara says it will take years for her to finish her studies (not next year).
B: The museum will have lots of foreign visitors, but Clara is not going abroad.
C: *… we'll have a special exhibition on African history at the museum, and that'll keep me very busy.*

p.26   LISTENING   Part Three

14 gym: *The swimming pool will be open on Monday and the gym and squash courts …*

15 Saturday: *a small delay with the indoor tennis court – so I'm afraid you'll have to wait for that till Saturday.*

16 215: *access to the Sports Centre for a whole year for £215.*

17 lessons: *you would have to pay extra for sports equipment … and also for swimming lessons.*

18 age: *don't forget to include your age and also your weight.*

19 Reysall: r-e-y-s-a-double l

p.27   LISTENING   Part Four

20 B: Lara says *I may have to give up the whole idea. And it would be such a pity …*

21 A: Jack says *when I was ten … there was nothing I liked more* (than acting).

22 B: When Jack says his voice is *not as good*, Lara says *Of course it is. It's improved.*

23 A: Jack says Lara had all the qualities, and he often wondered why she had not become an actor.

24 A: Jack says *I'll do that.*

25 B: Lara says *Oh, that would disappoint everyone. I can't do that.*

p.28   SPEAKING   Part One

FURTHER PRACTICE AND GUIDANCE (p.29)

A Detailed Study

There are many possible ways to give a full answer. These are only examples of what you might say.
2   I will use it in my work and in my studies.
3   I saw a very good film.
4   There are many beautiful places to walk in my town.
I like walking in the hills near my house.

TEST TWO

p.34   READING   Part One

1   **B:** *take your rubbish with you* (do not leave it in the area)

2   **C:** Amanda paid for 2 days instead of just one, *send me a cheque … you owe me*

3   **A:** George has to telephone his boss (*Your boss … call her this afternoon …*)

4   **C:** *Visitors are welcome to watch* (to see how the monkeys are fed)

5   **B:** *Show this advert and get 10% discount.*

p.36   READING   Part Two

6   **B:** *full of danger and excitement* (a thriller), *wonderful descriptions of the towns …* (read about interesting cities), *five hundred pages …* (wants a long book)
F is also a thriller, but there are no descriptions of places (all in a hotel).

7   **H:** *… by one of America's most widely-read novelists …* (well-known authors), *will bring tears to your eyes* (a novel that will make her cry), *… it can be read in a day…* (no patience with long books)
B is wrong, it will take days to read and she doesn't want a detective story this time. D is wrong as it is a long story and it is funny.

8   **G:** *… a young man's voyage across the Atlantic* (about dangerous journeys), *illustrated with beautiful drawings …* (wants a book that has pictures), *will sometimes make you laugh …* (books with a funny side)
E is wrong because it is about a journey in the future. A is wrong because it's not about a journey.

9   **E:** *… travels into the future in a time machine* (science fiction), *You will not be able to guess how it all finishes …* (unexpected ending)
C is wrong, it is science fiction but you know how it will end.

10   **A:** *a 19th century couple and their small sons …* (describes how children lived in the past) *To enjoy it fully, read it when you have lots of time* (a novel to read on holiday).
E is wrong, it's about children in the future. D is wrong, the people are childhood friends, not children.

p.40   READING   Part Three

11   **B:** *It has continued to grow ever since.*

12   **B:** *There are no requirements or entrance exams …*

13   **A:** *new members are not allowed to miss practice sessions*

14   **A:** *new members are welcome throughout the year*

15   **B:** *… and learn how they were created.* (They will not create their own music.)

16   **A:** *… Tours both in the UK and abroad …*

17   **A:** *… songs everyone knows, … as well as less well-known pieces*

18   **A:** *Full-time Students £68 per year, … must bring their college or … when they register.*

19   **B:** *… even if members have personal copies …*

20   **B:** *contact the Membership Secretary … or visit our website*

p.42   READING   Part Four

21   **C:** *a demanding job and a family … I don't live in luxury … training has to fit around everything else in my life*
A: She says her life *is exciting*. It is sometimes difficult, but she does not complain.

B: She mentions her training, but does not describe a programme.
D: She does not give any advice to runners.

22 B: *I hurt my left knee while running.*
A: Her daughter was four but she *was managing fine*
C: She had gone to college before that.
D: fitting in a full-time job *was not easy*, but she was *managing fine*.

23 D: *work part-time until midday*
A: She mentions more training but does not mention weekends.
B: She wants to work fewer hours, not give up her job.
C: leaving work at midday because *there will be more training to do*, she may get somebody to help with the housework.

24 A: Her employers are *understanding*, so she does not work at weekends.
B: There is no mention of giving up running.
C: Her employers don't mind her changing her running shoes and tracksuit, but they do not pay for that.
D: No, they allow her not to work weekends.

25 B: *I won the Dublin Marathon and the European Games.* Her hard work is mentioned several times: *fitting in a full-time job, family and running … training has to fit around everything else.*
A: She has *pressures of family and work* but she has also won some important competitions.
C: She says she was *managing fine* as a mother.
D: She does not say she would like the luxury, she only says her life is different.

p.44   READING   Part Five

26 C: *who* refers to *people*; *which* is for things / objects; *whose* has a possessive meaning

27 A: an event *takes* place; you *hold* an event

28 B: you *develop* a skill; you *become* skilful / good at something; your skills *grow* (become better)

29 C: *have + to*; *must* and *may* + infinitive without *to*; *have got to.*

30 D: *share* with; *inform/talk* about

31 D: *like me* is used because the writer is comparing himself to the reader

32 A: *experience* in this use is uncountable, so you need *much*; a *lot* of, *many* and *few* are countable.

33 B: *by the end* means when the challenge was coming to an end

34 B: you *meet* new people; *introduce* people to others; *get to know* people (learn more about them); *greet* people (say hello)

35 A: *thinking* is the only word that goes with *of*

p.45   WRITING   Part One

1   The new restaurant **belongs** to a very rich man.

2   A famous architect **designed** The Bluebell.

3   Other restaurants in the area are not so **comfortable as** The Bluebell.

4   The Bluebell **has** got English and French dishes on its menu.

5   Meal prices at The Bluebell will be the same **(up) until/(up) till/up to** 30 August.

p.46   WRITING   Part Two

Question 6
Model Answer

> Hello, Sarah!
> I'm in Seville, a lovely city. I came by train from Madrid. I'm staying in a small hotel in the centre. I want to see everything, but I only have four days. This afternoon I'll go to a museum.
> Love
> Lisa

FURTHER PRACTICE AND GUIDANCE (p.47)

A Detailed Study

1
a) Yes. It is only 22 words. This answer does not cover the points appropriately.
b) Yes, but it does not give enough information about each point. This is not a good answer.
c) No, it is 45 words. You should always try to write about this number of words.
d) Yes, and it covers them appropriately and fully.
e) Yes, it is much better because the writer has included some interesting information about each point.

2
A   The first point is missing (how you travelled).
B   The second point is missing (where in the city you are staying).

p.48 WRITING Part Three

Question 7
Model answer

> *Dear Pam*
>
> *It was a lovely surprise to get a letter from you! You asked me about museums. I love history museums which have lots of interesting things from the past, like coins and the clothes people used to wear. I also like museums about animals and wildlife.*
>
> *In my city there is a museum called 'The Transport Museum', where you can see how people travelled a hundred years ago. It has very old buses and trains and you can get on them and sit in the driver's seat. There is also a Furniture Museum, with chairs and tables from the 18th and 19th centuries, but I think it is a bit boring.*
>
> *That's all for now. Write again soon!*
>
> *Love*
>
> *X*

Your letter answers your friend's questions and
- it is well organized: 1. you mention your friend's letter 2. you say what type of museum you like 3. you give information about museums in your area
- it shows a good range of tenses / grammar / linking words: *which have/like coins/used to wear/ see how/you can/There is also/but*
- it shows good use of vocabulary: *surprise/ interesting/the past/coins/clothes/wildlife/transport/ centuries*
- it has good opening and closing sentences: *It was a lovely surprise to get a letter from you!/That's all for now. Write again soon!*

Question 8
Model answer

> *Mark wanted to visit a friend , so he got on a bus. His friend's name was Angelo. Mark wanted to arrive quickly because he had to give Angelo an important letter from a girl.*
>
> *Mark sat down and opened the window. Suddenly there was a strong wind and the letter flew out. Mark quickly got off the bus. He ran after the letter, but then he had to stop at a traffic light. Where was the letter? He decided to run along the street again. He ran and ran and then he saw the letter, still flying in the wind. Then a young man caught it in his hand. Mark realized that the young man was Angelo and that he was in front of Angelo's house!*

This is a good story and
- it is well organized: 1. why he was visiting his friend (had a letter for him) 2. what happened on the bus (the letter flew out of the window) 3. what he did (he went after it) 4. how it ended (Angelo got the letter)

- it shows a good range of tenses / grammar / linking words: *had to give/sat down/got off/ran/ but/decided to/caught it/realized*
- it shows good use of vocabulary: *important/strong wind/traffic light/flying*
- it has a good closing sentence: *Mark realized that the young man was Angelo and that he was in front of Angelo's house!*

p.49 LISTENING Part One

1 A: *Next* week the gallery will open at 9.30, not this weekend.
   B:10.15 is the normal opening hour *at weekends*.
   C: *The gallery will open at a quarter past eleven.*

2 A: The woman says *a pizza is too much*.
   B: *The salad sounds great. I'll have some too. ... A bowl of soup and a roll. That'll be enough for me.*
   C: When the man says the ice-cream is really good, the woman says *maybe next time* (not today).

3 **A:** *I'll never put it under my chair again* (but this time she did).
   B: The woman says the best place is on a chair, where she can keep an eye on it, but that's an idea for the future.
   C: The man suggests that in future she should hang it from the back of her chair.

4 A: The man explains that he usually walks, and adds *but I was carrying a heavy briefcase*.
   B: *Yesterday I got on it* (he means the bus) *at 8.15.*
   C: The woman says *it was silly not to take one* (a taxi). Silly that he did not take a taxi.

5 A: The woman says *we've got an old table – so that can wait*. The man says *let's get what we need most*.
   B: The woman mentions the chest of drawers first but then she agrees about the sofa – *it must come first*.
   C: *You're right about the sofa, though. It must come first.*

6 A: Woman 2 says that she will start taking lessons soon.
   B: The two women will swim in the evening, after the cinema.
   C: Woman 1: *We could have a swim then (in the evening), after the cinema*. Woman 2: *OK ...*

7 A: These are the weather conditions in the hills, not the seaside.
   B: *The wind has brought a large amount of cloud to this area* (the seaside) *... we won't see the sun ...*
   C: The reporter says *we won't see the sun here for the rest of the day.*

p.52 LISTENING Part Two

8 A: His mother encouraged him but he chose to do it.
B: *It was good for the practical side of my course, so I took the job.*
C: *I didn't really need it*

9 A: *which were always kept more or less the same, – not a real challenge for me.*
B: The manager did not like it when Patrick left, but he was not unfriendly.
C: Patrick says he only worked from 5 till 10 p.m., which was great.

10 A: His recipes were *like in no other Italian restaurant.*
B: *the owner said I had to find cheaper ingredients. And I managed to do that …*
C: Patrick does not say that the owner created menus.

11 A: He says his chicken recipes are not as good as the recipes of his friend.
B: He is not happy with his vegetable recipes yet.
C: *I think I've produced some of the best.*

12 A: *Nothing's more important … than the ability to pay attention to what cooks and customers are saying … This is a skill many chefs lack.*
B: *All chefs are great cooks.*
C: *keeping up-to-date … I think we all do that.*

13 A: He says they can find the right job after school.
B: *Work hard … but give yourself time for other things.*
C: *Get to know them and interview them* (other chefs).

FURTHER PRACTICE AND GUIDANCE (p.53)

A Detailed Study

1 a) We know that this is True without listening: Patrick *accepted* his first job.
b) We know that this is False without listening: What did he *dislike* about …
c) We can't answer this without listening: It is option C in Question 9.
d) We can't answer this without listening: It is option C in Question 10.
e) We know that this is False without listening: Patrick thinks that *his best recipes …*
f) We can't answer this without listening: this is option B in Question 12.
g) We know that this is True without listening: What does Patrick *advise …*

2 a) *just to learn new dishes*
b) He was unhappy because Patrick decided to give up the job.
c) to find cheaper ingredients
d) They are not as good as his friend's.
e) *All of them: I think we all do that*
f) Find out useful information.

p.54 LISTENING Part Three

14 **the dining room**: *I'll come and see you all in the dining room. Please be there at 9 o'clock.*

15 **9.15**: *we'll be off at 9.15.*

16 **forest**: *stop for an hour in the forest, to have a picnic lunch.*

17 **village**: *You may want to have a look at a village …*

18 **boat**: *or take a boat trip*

19 **(sun) hat**: *so don't forget a hat. It's important.*

p.55 LISTENING Part Four

20 B: Diana says *It can be dangerous … But I was there with a guide, and he said it was OK …*

21 B: James says *Why do people say … It's so untrue.*

22 A: Diana says she told her parents *thinking they'd disapprove, but they were very encouraging.*

23 A: *It was so much simpler than I'd imagined!*

24 B: Diana offers to have a look at the list of courses, but does not suggest a person to teach James.

25 A: Diana says she will do it this time, but not every year.

p.56 SPEAKING Part One

1 Your answer must be in the future tense, e.g. *In the morning I'll play tennis with my friends and in the evening I'll go to a party.*

2 Your answer must be in the simple present tense, e.g. *I go twice a month/every Saturday, I don't go very often. I do/don't like the cinema very much.*

3 Your answer must be in the present, e.g. *Pasta is my favourite food, I like beef most, I have it once a week.*

4 You must use *like + -ing*, e.g. *I like watching television and listening to music.*

5 Extend your answer, e.g. *Yes, I do, I really like computers. I like playing games on my computer.*

6 Your answer must be in the simple past tense, e.g. *I went to the seaside and I enjoyed it very much. I stayed in a lovely hotel.*

TEST THREE

p.62   READING   Part One

1 **B:** Janet says: *If that's no good for you, call her today.*

2 **C:** *smoking is not allowed in any part of the train*

3 **B:** Dr Rawlin is not sure about the spelling of the lecturer's name.

4 **C:** *give up your seat to …* means offer them your seat

5 **C:** *buy two … get a third … free*

p.64   READING   Part Two

6 **B:** Animals are *free in open fields* (not in cages); *Easy access by public transport* (Simon hasn't got a car); *wonderful surroundings* (area of natural beauty)
F is wrong, not an area of natural beauty (in the heart of the city), does not say if the animals are in cages.

7 **E:** *collections of paintings, books and furniture* (an art exhibition); *tour the gardens* (a walk in the open air); *great gifts* (present for friend)
D is wrong, sculptures not for sale.
H is wrong, not possible to combine it with a walk.

8 **G:** *marine creatures and sea plants* (he is a biology teacher); *informative video* (something that he may use in class with his students)
C is wrong, it is open only in the afternoon and there is nothing to buy for his students.
B is wrong, he would need a day to see it.

9 **C:** *story of mountains … Ice Age* (learn about effects of climate change on earth); *lectures by experts* (attend an interesting talk)
F is wrong, a talk is mentioned but it is for children.

10 **A:** *glass makers … watch them while they turn …* (prefers to see them at work); *open weekends* (he wants an activity for Saturday), *buy a unique vase* (buy something for his house)
D is wrong, he can't see the sculptors at work, the sculptures are not for sale.

p.66   READING   Part Three

11 **A:** *be able to walk for at least two hours at a time*

12 **A:** *have an opportunity to work on the projects* (to improve the area for the birds)

13 **B:** You can't choose, you stay *with local New Zealanders*, and in cabins only during the *overnight guided trip.*

14 **B:** the text says that the place is *little known outside* of New Zealand, not in New Zealand.

15 **B:** *Depending on the weather, the programme will include …*

16 **A:** *Waterproof jackets … are essential items which cannot be bought locally.*

17 **B:** *Upon receipt of the form we will check the availability we have for the programme you have chosen …*

18 **A:** *Please note that we will return your deposit if you decide not to go.*

19 **B:** *… needs to be paid to us eight weeks before you start the programme.*

20 **B:** *… travel insurance for the whole of your journey, as we do not provide that service.*

FURTHER PRACTICE AND GUIDANCE (p.68)

A Detailed Study

1 **a)** *up to two hours* means at least two hours

2 **b)** *not only … but also* means this and <u>also</u> this

3 **a)** *staying in forest cabins* means will stay in forest cabins

4 **a)** *outside New Zealand* means not in New Zealand.

5 **b)** *the activities depend on the weather*, i.e. will only take place if the weather is suitable

6 **a)** *cannot be bought* means you cannot buy

7 **b)** *upon receipt* means as soon as (when) we receive

8 **b)** if you decide not to go because you change your mind

9 **b)** (money) *to be paid to us* means you have to pay us

10 **a)** *arrange your own* means be responsible for.

p.70 READING PART FOUR

21 **C:** *it is a great chance to explore their interests.* The second paragraph is all about ideas on how to find a summer job.
A: He mentions that summer jobs are low-paid, but he says there are many other advantages.
B: He describes his own summer job as an example, but does not describe any other jobs.
D: He does not offer summer jobs, he only tells students how to find them.

22 **D:** *email the manager to ask what temporary jobs exist … is what I recommend*
A: The writer says colleges advertise jobs, but he does not advise students to ask colleges for help.
B: The writer mentions ads in newspapers, but he does not say it is the best option.
C: The writer mentions organizations, but he does not say they are his preferred option.

23 **A:** *… uninteresting because my responsibilities were not clear*
B: He says he started enjoying the job when he had more projects.
C: One of the projects was on research, and that's when he started enjoying it.
D: He mentions *creating web pages,* which means he does have computer skills.

24 **C:** *I decided to train as a teacher rather than a researcher when I got back.*
A: He had *enough to cover … daily needs* and *no financial worries,* but he was not saving money.
B: He mentions schools, but he does not mention people he met.
D: His only regret is that he did not learn much about the United States.

25 **B:** *However, few students know what jobs may be available.*
A: He says *a good summer job seldom leaves you much free time and you should be prepared for that.*
C: He says employers are interested in doing this.
D: He says there is *little financial reward,* but he thinks there are many other advantages in taking a summer job.

p.72 READING Part Five

26 **D:** *go into; attend/visit* a school (without *to*); *appear in* or *at* a place

27 **B:** you are *paid for* your work (you get the money); you are *charged for* something (you have to pay); you are *owed* money (somebody has money which is yours); you are *fined* (you have to pay a fine)

28 **A:** people of different *ages*; different *times* of day; people born many *years* ago; the *date* when you were born

29 **C:** *No … at all* are needed (means you *don't* need *any … at all.* What qualifications do you need? None.

30 **C:** *must* (without *to*), *ought / have / need + to,*

31 **D:** *become* a doctor / teacher; *turn into* a beautiful woman; *train as* a … ; *work as* a …

32 **A:** *hear about/of* something; *listen to* something; *be informed about* something; *be told about* something

33 **B:** *makes* it hard(er) means it is harder; it *gets* harder

34 **C:** People *shouldn't do … unless they like* children, if people *don't like* children, they *should not do* this job

35 **D:** *miss* somebody; *lack* something (not have); the children *leave* for a holiday; *lose* something (can't find it)

p.73 WRITING Part One

1 Last year there **were** more than 500 students at the King School.

2 I asked at Reception: How much **does/will/would** a conversation course cost?

3 The price of the course **includes** the coursebook.

4 The King School is the **least** expensive of all schools in town.

5 Students are not allowed to attend classes **unless/until** they have paid the fee.

p.74 WRITING Part Two

Question 6
Model answer

> Hello, Peter
> Thank you so much for the picture of your town. I like the old buildings! I will put it on a wall in my bedroom.
> Would you like to come and visit me in July? I'll have free time then.
> Yours
> Patricio

Your card covers all the points:
- you have thanked Peter for the present: *Thank you so much for the picture of your town*
- you have said what you will do with it: *I will put it on a wall in my bedroom.*
- you have suggested when Peter could visit you: *Would you like to come and visit me in July?*

p.75 WRITING Part Three

Question 7
See Further Practice and Guidance, page 76, for a model answer.

Question 8
Model answer

> **The castle on the hill**
>
> *Last year I went on holiday with a friend. We stayed in a tent near a river. One day we saw that there was an old castle on a high hill, and we asked a man if we could visit it. He told us not to do it because there was a dangerous criminal there. But we decided to go.*
>
> *It was a difficult climb. We walked into the castle. Suddenly, we saw a very old woman with a kind face. 'Would you like some tea?', she said. 'I seldom get visitors.' I asked her: 'Why do people say you are a criminal?' 'It's a long story. I'll tell you if you visit me again', she said. One day I will go back to the castle.*

This is good story:
- it is well organized: 1. where you were when you saw the castle 2. why you wanted to visit it 3. what happened in the castle
- it shows a good range of tenses / grammar / linking words: *went on holiday/stayed/saw/asked a man if/told us not to/because/decided to/seldom get/I'll tell you*

- it shows good use of vocabulary: *tent/high/dangerous/criminal/climb/suddenly/visitors*
- it has good opening and closing sentences: *Last year I went on holiday with a friend./One day I will go back to the castle.*

FURTHER PRACTICE AND GUIDANCE (p.76)

A Detailed Study

1
a) X (the letter should be about <u>your</u> hobby, not about a programme, but you could mention a programme, e.g. *I started collecting stones when I saw a programme on TV.*)

b) ✔

c) ✔

d) X (If you don't have any hobbies, invent one or choose the other question.)

e) ✔

f) X (the letter is about <u>your</u> hobby, but you could mention that your sister likes the same hobby)

g) ✔

h) ✔

i) X (be careful, this is about your hobby and not about your free time in general)

j) ✔ (if this is your hobby)

2
1 C 2 A 3 B

p.77 LISTENING Part One

1 A: The man wants to give him CDs, but he then agrees the lamp is a good idea.
   B: *How about a lamp for his desk? ... That's not a bad idea ... Can you buy it?*
   C: The man rejects the tie idea because it is too personal.

2 A: She has long blonde hair but she no longer wears glasses.
   B: This is what she used to look like in the past.
   C: *She no longer wears glasses ... Her hair's now blonde. She's had it long for ...*

3 A: This idea is rejected because it would be a very different kind of party.
   B: *I said we could have it in my house ... invite fewer people and ... as we'd planned*
   C: This idea is rejected because it would be a very different kind of party.

4   A: She says she will start buying it, she is not reading it regularly yet.
B: *It's the one magazine I read as soon as it comes on Tuesdays.*
C: She says she only reads it when she has time, she often throws it away unread.

5   A: *start with an opera evening … no charge for this first event …*
B: The ticket prices for the Youth Orchestra are £25.
C: The ticket prices for the rock concert are £25.

6   A: Brenda says she gets up by 7.30.
B: *Could you call me tomorrow at a quarter past eight, please, if that isn't too early for you …*
C: 10.15 is the time the conversation is taking place.

7   A: He wanted to watch TV, but the lights went off.
B: His telephone conversation had finished when the lights went off.
C: *I started making myself some supper … That's when it all went dark.*

p.80   LISTENING   Part Two

8   A: *completely black* refers to the Madagascar *indri*
B: It was filmed in *one of the least visited areas.*
C: *we hardly ever get to see any of them* (animals), *which is a pity.*

9   A: *you should prepare yourselves for a very unexpected conclusion.*
B: the best drama series for ages
C: *excellent performances* (from both actors)

10 A: It is the same actor as five years ago.
B: *… was funnier when he first started, five years ago*
C: *for all the family*

11 A: *… will be at 8.30 instead of 10.30.*
B: *a change on BBC 2* refers to the time, not the channel.
C: The programme is *the best for a long time*, it did not take a long time to make.

12 A: It is *based on a novel*, not real life.
B: It is not original, rather it is *similar to* lots of *other detective stories.*
C: *… the quality of the acting makes it special*

13 A: Two young women are mentioned, but it does not say they are the only ones.
B: *I don't think there's enough … to keep young audiences interested*
C: It is about students in the city of London, but this is not the problem.

p.81   LISTENING   Part Three

14 **Monday(s)**: *they'll all … on Mondays*

15 **post office**: *facing the post office, next to the museum.*

16 **18 February**: *Both of them begin on 18 February.*

17 **violin**: *a choice between learning to play the piano or the violin.*

18 **photo(graph)**: *the other is called 'What Makes a Good Photograph'?*

19 **(course) books**: *You'll have to pay for the course books separately.*

FURTHER PRACTICE AND GUIDANCE (p.82)

Detailed Study

1   a) a teacher
    b) leisure courses
    c) Probably about the content of the courses, the times, the teachers, the prices, the classrooms.

2
14 j
15 e
16 c
17 h
18 a
19 b

p.83   LISTENING   PART FOUR

20 B: Nora is sure she wants an office job, even if it is not exciting: *That's why I want a job like that.*

21 A: He learnt about organizing meetings: *It certainly wasn't a waste of time.*

22 B: Sam says he'd quite like a job where he had nothing to do except computer work.

23 A: Sam says *I don't speak it as well as you do.* Nora says, *Your German's excellent*, but the question asks about Sam's opinion, not Nora's.

24 B: Sam doesn't mind that he will get less pay, Nora will look at the money first.

25 B: Nora thanks him for the offer but says she can manage without his help

p.84   SPEAKING   Part One

1   Your answer may be in the future tense, e.g. *I'll go out with my friends* or you can use *may* to show you are not sure, e.g. *I don't know, I may go out with my friends or I may stay at home and read.*

2   If you have a favourite sport: *Tennis is my favourite sport/I like tennis most. I play every day.* If you don't like sport: *I don't practise any sport, but I like to watch football.*

3   Your answer must be in the present and you need to use expressions like: *once/ twice/three times a week/month; every day/Saturday/evening* Or you can say: *I never watch TV, I seldom watch TV, I don't watch TV very often.*

4   You must use *like + -ing*, and give a reason, e.g. *I like shopping for clothes, I think it is fun.* Or: *I don't like shopping. I think it is boring/There are too many people in the shops.*

5   Your answer must be in the simple past tense, e.g. *I had a great party. I invited all my friends.* Or: *I didn't celebrate it. I never celebrate my birthday.*

6   You must use *would* in your answer, e.g. *I'd like to learn Italian because I want to travel in Italy.*

FURTHER PRACTICE AND GUIDANCE (p.87)

A Detailed Study
1   tent
2   rucksack
3   sleeping-bag
4   thermos / thermos flask
5   towel
6   walking boots

TEST FOUR

p.90　READING　Part One

1　**C:** will start earlier than usual: *from 9 to 10.30 instead of the usual 9.30 to 10.30.*

2　**B:** offering Greg theatre tickets: *If you want them, come to …*

3　**B:** *Do not use … if bottle top is broken*, means the same as only use … if the bottle top is unbroken

4　**A:** George is going out *to get us* (Adriana and himself) *some steak*

5　**B:** *Get it today or they'll lend it to …*

p.92　READING　Part Two

6　**F:** *within walking distance of the railway station* (need to be near train or bus services), *breakfast, lunch and dinner* (all meals included), *area good for riding … tours to see birds.* (horse-riding and see some wildlife)
A is wrong as only breakfast provided. B is wrong as it can be reached only by car.

7　**D:** *only ten minutes on foot from the city's theatre area* (no more than a fifteen minute walk …) *several good quality restaurants nearby* (have dinner in different places), *near theatre area* (wants to go to concerts and plays)
E is wrong, too far from the attractions and it has only one restaurant nearby. C is wrong, it is 10 km from a village.

8　**A:** *peaceful location* (a quiet place), *horses available for hire* (ride horses), *kitchen for guests to use* (cook their own meals), *good 24-hour bus service* (then go into the city for a drink)
B is wrong, no horses and difficult access to the city centre. F is wrong, they can't cook their own meals.

9　**C:** *valley in the hills* (in or near the hills) *the owner, an expert in mountain climbing …* (needs an experienced guide), *free access to internet services* (needs to use email)
B is wrong, no internet access. F is wrong, no guide for his walks.

10　**H:** *only a ten-minute drive from the city* (drive to the city in under fifteen minutes) *away from the traffic and noise* (a quiet place), *parking space behind the hotel* (with a car park), *breakfast and dinner can be served …* (dinner at the hotel), *it has a swimming pool* (a swimming pool for their children)
A is wrong, only breakfast provided. D is wrong, meals are not provided.

p.94　READING　Part Three

11　**A:** *… the history of women inventors in this period is very long.*

12　**B:** *… she was made to work in a cotton factory by her parents.*

13　**A:** *… fix the machine so … the same fault again, straight away the machine would shut down completely.*

14　**A:** *… to be finally recognized as the owner of the idea.*

15　**A:** *… women were not encouraged to be business people any more than they were encouraged to be inventors.*

16　**B:** *… she would usually sell it to somebody for not much cash …*

17　**B:** *… working out how to fix the covers so that they would not fly away on windy days was difficult, but she managed to do it.*

18　**B:** *'The biggest umbrella men in the country told me it could not be done.'*

19　**B:** *But for someone with such a long career, surprisingly little is known about …*

20　**A:** *… she was always honest about her lack of such skills.*

p.96　READING　Part Four

21　**C:** *accompanying a postman, every day he …, one of the longest … in the world*
A: He says it is long, difficult and expensive, but he does not ask for support.
B: He mentions the wild landscape, but this is not his main purpose.
D: There are dangerous animals below, but his purpose is not to warn about dangers to the postman.

22　**A:** *To help with the cost, the plane takes three or four paying local people or tourists.*
B: People pay 50 cents to <u>send</u> a letter to the outback (or to any other place in Australia) not to have it delivered to them.
C: He says the system is expensive, but does not mention a different system.
D: The sender pays the same (50 cents) for a letter to the outback or to a neighbouring town.

23　**B:** *this looks no more exciting than the post delivered to me in England.*
A: He expects to see special items, but there are not any.
C: He looks at the names, but doesn't say he can't read them.
D: There is a pile of post, but he doesn't say it's disorganized.

24 D: *I do miss actually going shopping.*
A: She says *there's not much that you can't get delivered.*
B: She looks forward to the weekly delivery but doesn't say she'd like it to be more frequent.
C: Rowan checks the time but Sandy does not complain about the length of the visit.

25 B: *sets off with his post bags in the tail of his little plane, hand-delivered by flying postman to …*
A: Rowan checks the time because he knows he has many other stops. It is the writer who talks to the local person, so this is not the case.
C: The post plane is very small, but it is large enough for a pile of post at the back and a few passengers.
D: The writer says both tourists and local inhabitants can be passengers.

FURTHER PRACTICE AND GUIDANCE (p.98)

A Detailed Study

1 c) The text refers to future problems: *avoid the problems we had …* There are no problems yet, but *this time they might be more serious.*
a: There is no complaint about present problems.
b: We know there were problems in the past, but no reasons are given.

2 b) *All the managers would need to do is …* Providing certain facilities is a suggestion for improvement.
a: The text begins with a description, but the purpose of the writer is not to describe.
c: Guests are mentioned, but the purpose is not to attract them.

3 a) *There is no better way …* is a way of encouraging and persuading students to travel.
b: Students are in the final year at school, but school travel is not mentioned.
c: Actual places to travel to are not mentioned.

p.99   READING   Part Five

26 B: *Although* here means he is very young, but he knows; *however* is normally followed by a comma: He is young. However, he knows …; *even* can be used to mean something similar to *although* but in this case requires the word *though* after it; *so* means as a result: He is young, so he doesn't know …

27 D: you *take* somebody to a place; *go* or *travel with* somebody; *carry* a child or a thing in your arms

28 C: when something *still* happens it has not stopped; *yet* means it has not happened up to now; *already* means something happened (in the past); *since* means from a particular date – here that it has not happened *since* 1999.

29 C: *asked* is followed by *for*; the other three are followed by *to*.

30 A: *says* does not need a person or pronoun after it; you *tell* or *inform* somebody; you *speak* to somebody.

31 B: you *lose* a job (e.g. when a factory closes), you *miss* a job when you think about a job you liked; you *give up* a job when you don't want it any longer; you *throw away* an object when you do not want it any longer.

32 B: *where* is used to refer to places; *when* for times; *which* for things; *who* for people.

33 D: *both* means the two of them; *either* means one or the other; *some* means a few of them; *any* means any one of several.

34 A: you *become* rich / a doctor / a celebrity / famous; you *turn into* a different person; you *work as* an engineer; you *apply for* a job as an engineer.

35 B: *hope* is followed by *to*; *dreams + of*; *believes* and *thinks* + (that) + pronoun.

FURTHER PRACTICE AND GUIDANCE (p.100)

A Detailed Study

The answers are explained in the key to Reading Part Five.

p.102   WRITING   Part One

1 People say that this is **the most interesting** castle in Europe.

2 The castle **has been** open to the public since last year.

3 Students **do not/don't** have to pay anything to visit the castle.

4 Mr Brandon always **meets** visitors at the door.

5 I asked Mr Brandon: **'Did you** live in the castle when you were a child?'

p.103 WRITING   Part Two

Question 6
Model answer

Hello Phil

I've joined a new sports club. It is only 10 minutes by bus from our school. I like it because it has a swimming pool, tennis courts, table tennis and a gym. I would like you to come too. You'll love it!

See you

X

Your email covers all the points:
- you have said where the club is: *It is only 10 minutes by bus from our school.*
- you have said why you like it: *because it has a swimming pool, tennis courts, table tennis and a gym*
- you have invited Phil to join: *I would like you to come too. You'll love it!*

p.104 WRITING   Part Three

Question 7
Model answer

Dear Mark

Thanks for your letter. You asked me my opinion about buying a mobile phone. I think it is a good idea because you can have contact with many people and you can use it to find help quickly. You can also send messages to friends. But be careful when you choose one. Some are not very good.

In my country lots of people use mobile phones and even small children have one. Young people use them more than older people. Some use it when they are driving but then the police may stop them and they may be in trouble.

Let me know if you decide to get one.

See you soon

X

The letter gives the information your friend needs and
- it is well-organized: 1. good idea 2. why it is a good idea 3. people in your country
- it shows a good range of tenses / grammar / linking words: *can/Be careful/use/may stop/ because/so/But/ and even/when*
- it shows good use of vocabulary: *contact/ messages/police/trouble*
- it has good opening and closing sentences: *Thank you for your letter/Let me know if you decide to buy one.*

See A Detailed Study below for the model answer to Question 8.

FURTHER PRACTICE AND GUIDANCE (p.105)

A Detailed Study
Question 8

1
a) When Carlos saw that the suitcase was empty, he went to the police.
   Carlos went to the police when he saw that the suitcase was empty.
b) Carlos saw that the suitcase was empty, so he went to the police.
c) As soon as Carlos saw that the suitcase was empty, he went to the police.
   Carlos went to the police as soon as he saw that the suitcase was empty.
d) Carlos went to the police because he saw that the suitcase was empty.
e) Carlos looked everywhere for his suitcase but he couldn't find it.
f) Even though/Though/Although Carlos looked everywhere for his suitcase, he couldn't find it.

2

The lost suitcase
Last night *was* a beautiful night. I *was having* dinner with my friends in a restaurant. Suddenly we *heard* a big shout: 'Hey!' We all *looked* at Paul. Paul shouted loudly: 'I've lost my suitcase!' Then he *ran* out of the restaurant. But Alan *stopped* him. Alan *said* to Paul: 'Keep calm, now you need to think carefully where you've been today.' After Paul *told* us, we *went* everywhere that he had been – library, café, bus stop, cinema … Finally we went to the car park and we found it! Paul opened it quickly but it was empty. A thief had taken all his clothes.

p.107 LISTENING Part One

1 **A:** ... *there wasn't a single piece I liked!*
B: He says it was just sandwiches, but nobody was expecting a big meal.
C: He says he enjoyed the party games, they were fun.

2 A: Nothing is said about booking for the guitar concert.
B: *This is a small theatre so book your tickets soon.*
C: Tickets are <u>only</u> available on the day.

3 **A:** *Why don't we get her a beach bag? Let's do that.*
B: Jill already has sun hat (she was wearing one).
C: They both agree that they should not give her a T-shirt again.

4 A: The rain will stop tonight.
B: It won't be sunny tomorrow, but the day after.
C: *... last of the rain tonight but it'll remain cloudy for the next twenty-four hours.*

5 A: She answered the phone, but she did not leave the present near the phone.
B: *I put it back down on there* (on the dining room table)
C: It's not in her bag, she says they'll have to go back and get it.

6 A: The shoe shop job has many good points, but she prefers the bookshop job.
B: She doesn't want to work on Saturday afternoons.
C: *At the bookshop I get ... but it's a ten-minute walk ... So I'm going for it.*

7 A: 1.15 was the time for the afternoon play, but at that time they are bringing tennis reports.
B: 2.15 is the normal time for the *World Music* programme, but today it is later.
C: *... at the later time of 3.15, after the news.*

p.110 LISTENING Part Two

8 A: *I was keen on lots of other sports*
B: *... a bicycle race in my village and I just wanted to take part ...*
C: *mountain biking – I believed – was not something I'd be good at ... knowing I'd probably be last ...*

9 A: He mentions training not his mother.
B: *She replied I'd be lucky to come third or fourth! She wanted me to win of course, but she didn't really believe I could do it.*
C: His mother is now a fan, but Philip does not say she encouraged other fans.

10 A: ... *wanting to interview me, but I go straight to where all my fans are.*
B: *I refuse to have conversations with them at this point.*
C: *I go straight to where all my fans are – they want autographs ... I'm always happy to do it.*

11 A: *I do a lot of really hard gym work – and I think this is it*
B: *... on difficult roads, as every other racer does.*
C: *we all ... make sure we have the best possible bikes.*

12 A: *... but hardly anything on actual races.*
B: *few of them actually buy magazines, so the publishers are always worrying about sales ...*
C: *... professional racers would find little of interest in them.*

13 A: *... it would take too much of my time.*
B: *... refused an offer to write a book ..., for the same reason ...*
C: *an offer to do TV advertisements ... now I need the income – and I think it'll be good for the sport*

p.111 LISTENING Part Three

14 **(sandy) beaches**: *sandy beaches which are among the most beautiful in the world.*

15 **70/seventy**: *an amazing variety of trees – well over seventy of them.*

16 **fan**: *air conditioning and a ceiling fan for your comfort*

17 **teabags/tea bags**: *Well, you'll have the opportunity to find out how they make them!*

18 **owner**: *you'll be able to talk to the owner*

19 **flight(s)**: *... but if you want me to arrange your flights ..., you have to pay for that separately.*

p.112 LISTENING Part Four

20 **A**: notice *good time* and *it'll be a great day.*

21 **B**: David had work *last weekend*, not this one.

22 **B**: notice *Now I think of it – it may be too late* (to get tickets).

23 **B**: Carol likes going to the cinema, but it is not David's *idea of fun.*

24 **A**: notice *not like you, I usually avoid sport ...*

25 **A**: notice *You'd be bored – I need a lot of practice – OK then.*

FURTHER PRACTICE AND GUIDANCE (p.113)

A Detailed Study

1 T: *good time/it'll be a great day*
2 T: *can't wait/last weekend writing a report*
3 F: *working at weekends is no fun/a bit of work to do*
4 F: David: *The Novo Band are here*
5 T: *Have you got yours?*
6 T: *may be too late*
7 T: *a great thriller … I saw it last week.*
8 F: *I heard about it.*
9 T: *not my idea of fun*
10 T: *usually avoid sport*
11 T: *Oh no, I'm only a beginner.*
12 F: *not that good myself*

p.114 SPEAKING Part One

1 Your answer should be in the present tense, e.g. *I like sports/fashion/computer/wildlife magazines* (give examples of magazines you read). *I usually borrow them from the library/I buy them every week/ A friend lends me her magazines.*

2 Your answer should be in the present tense, e.g. *I do/go/study/ watch/I (don't) like doing …/ I sometimes/often go … On Saturdays I … In the evenings I …*

3 Give reasons, e.g. *I always have a good time/I like action films/I go with my friends.* Add information: *I went to the cinema on Saturday and I saw …*

4 Give reasons, e.g. *I'd like to visit France because I'd like to see Paris and learn French.*

5 Your answer must be in the past tense, e.g. *My favourite food was pasta.* Add information: *I wanted to have it every day but my mother didn't let me.*

6 Your answer should be in the past tense, e.g. *(I started learning English) when I was five/when I was at school/in 2001/five years ago.*

LISTENING SCRIPTS

TEST ONE   PART ONE

Example:
Which musical instrument will the man buy?

Man: My daughter will be 12 next Saturday, and I've promised her a musical instrument. She thinks she's going to get a piano!

Woman: Oh dear. That's expensive, and then she might not play it very often. Why not get her a guitar, or a trumpet? There's always time to get her a piano when she's a bit older …

Man: No, I'll get her what she wants. I don't think she'd like a trumpet. And she's already got a guitar. She's quite good at it.

1   What will the woman wear at the party?

Woman: You know that dress we saw in the shop, the long one with short sleeves? May be I'll get it and wear it to Anna's party …

Man: You hardly ever wear long dresses, or even long skirts! You always say they're so uncomfortable. Why not wear your nice black trousers? They'd go well with your new blouse.

Woman: That's true, but it's a long-sleeved blouse, and it'll be very warm. A dress may not be as comfortable as trousers, but it'll look nicer.

Man: OK. When do you want to get it?

2   Where will Charles meet Bob?

Machine: This is Bob's answerphone. Please leave a message.

Charles: Hi, Bob. It's Charles here. About the cinema tonight. I'll have to work until about 6, so I'll just make it in time for the film. Can you be there earlier and get the tickets? There won't be enough time for a snack at the coffee house first as we'd planned, but let's meet there anyway. Better than you waiting for me in the street. Anyway, I'll walk across the park to avoid the crowds, so I hope to see you no later than 6.15. Bye!

3   When is the lecture?

Student 1: Is Professor Brown's lecture on the 23rd of March, as we were told? Somebody said it's changed.

Student 2: It has. Professor Brown has a meeting that day, so the lecture's now going to be on the 21st, same time.

Student 1: Oh, what a pity, I won't be able to make it, I've got lots of work to finish. I could make a later date, towards the end of the month …

Student 2: Well, we suggested the 31st, because it's a Friday, but the lecture room wasn't free then.

4   What did the man borrow from the library?

Man: I'm really disappointed. I wanted to get two videos from the library, to watch at the weekend, but they only allow you to take out one!

Woman: Well, that seems fair to me. There aren't that many videos. And I don't think you're allowed to borrow more than two books or CDs, isn't that right?

Man: Yes. I seldom borrow CDs, though, I've got quite a collection. Anyway, I knew one video wasn't enough for a long weekend, so I also got a couple of novels that sounded interesting.

5   How did the man learn about the cycling race?

Man: Hi, Jane, I was going to call you on your mobile. Have you heard about the cycling race next week? Ten miles across country, to the next village.

Woman: Really? I usually hear about these things on the local radio, but not this time.

Man: Well, that's how I learnt about it, in the ten o'clock sports news. I'm sure we'll get more information in the newspaper tomorrow. If you're interested, I'll phone you with the details when I get them.

Woman: Oh, yes. Thank you for letting me know.

6   What did they watch on TV yesterday?

Woman: You know, we missed a really good programme last night. While we had Channel 4 on for the news, on BBC 2 they were showing a programme about African wildlife! Pity we had no idea! And there's nothing really interesting on this evening, not really.

Man: I thought there was a good thriller at 9.

Woman: Yes, *Officer Brown*, which we've already seen. Months ago, remember? About the policeman who spent years following a suspect.

Man: Oh, yes, I remember now. Well, we may want to see it again.

7   Which activity can people under 14 do alone?

Woman: The Adventure Club offers a number of exciting sports and people who stay with us usually want to try them all. This is an ideal area for mountain climbing, of course. If you're under 14, however, you won't be able to do this by yourselves. The same is true of windsurfing – you'll be accompanied by one of our guides for your own safety. Horse riding is a favourite, and you can do it on your own. We've got enough horses for all of you, whenever you want them.

TEST ONE   PART TWO

Host: My guest today is Clara Thomas, who has an interesting job in the Museum of History. Clara, did you always want to work in a museum?

Clara: Hello. Oh, no, at school, most of my mates wanted to be lawyers and I was dreaming of being a teacher … When my best friend got a small part in a film – not my favourite job – I thought she was so lucky – at 15 she had the job she wanted! I wanted to go to college, to study history. Then I saw this museum job advertised.

Host: So you decided to apply …

Clara: Well … They wanted someone to organize the museum collections – for example, old coins, or ancient vases … very valuable pieces – it was a big responsibility, but that's what I wanted. I didn't apply immediately, though. I was afraid it wouldn't be interesting working on my own … with no-one to talk to. It took me two weeks to decide to apply. My mother was very upset!

Host: And you got the job!

Clara: Yes, I'll never forget my first day. I was introduced to all my colleagues. They were very friendly. One of them read a little speech she'd written to welcome me. Then somebody said there were some big boxes full of museum objects for me downstairs, could I go and get them? I couldn't believe it! I didn't say anything, I just did it! They were very heavy!

Host: Was everything else easier?

Clara: Not really. I had worked with computers, and this was very useful. I'm not very good with numbers, though, and as part of my job I had to look at objects the museum wanted to buy – usually from private collectors. For that you need an understanding of basic mathematics. My boss said I definitely should do something about it, and I did. I had to give up my French studies to make time for that.

Host: So what part of your job do you enjoy most?

Clara: I spend a lot of time writing short histories of museum objects – what they look like, where they were found … I find this research work much more exciting than preparing an important exhibition. I'm always afraid people might not like an exhibition! I don't get much of a chance to talk to visitors, but I like reading the comments they write in our visitors' book.

Host: Well, you're doing a great job. Any plans for the future?

Clara: Yes. I must make some progress with my history studies. But it'll take me years to get my degree because I'm studying part-time now. Next year will be exciting – we'll have a special exhibition on African history at the museum, and that'll keep me very busy. We'll have lots of visitors from all over the world.

Host: Clara, thank you for talking to us.

TEST ONE   PART THREE

Max: Hello. My name's Max and I'm the manager. Thank you for coming along today to visit our new Sports Centre. In a few minutes I'll take you round to see it. But first some information about the facilities we've got and when you can start using them.

The swimming pool will be open on Monday and the gym and squash courts will be ready for use on Wednesday. But we've had a small delay with the indoor tennis court – so I'm afraid you'll have to wait for that till Saturday. The good news is we're open every day, including Sunday.

Now, something about prices. The system we have is very flexible, so you can pay daily if you want to. However, you may want to think of paying a monthly fee, which is £35, or you can have access to the Sports Centre for a whole year for £215. We also give a special £50 discount for children under 10 years of age. Our prices include the use of all the facilities in the Sports Centre, but of course you would have to pay extra for sports equipment – racquets for example – and also for swimming lessons.

Registering to become a member of the Club is very easy. At Reception you'll find a membership form. Fill it in, and don't forget to include your age and also your weight – this is very important to see your level of fitness. We'll prepare a membership card for you, so please bring a photograph.

I could answer any questions now, but I'm sure you're all eager to go and have a look at the facilities. If you think of any other questions later though, call our secretary, Mrs Reysall, that is R - E - Y - S - A - DOUBLE L on 467 9900. She'll be very pleased to help you. Let's go then.

TEST ONE   PART FOUR

Lara: Hello Jack, good to see you. I was just going to call you. You know the play I'm preparing with my class? Would you be able to play one of the roles? One of my actors has dropped out …

Jack: Why me? I haven't been in a play for years.

Lara: Well, unless I find somebody soon, I may have to give up the whole idea. And it would be such a pity, all my students are so keen … Oh, come on, I thought you loved acting …

Jack: When I was about ten, yes, I did. There was nothing I liked more than performing in front of friends and family and being the centre of attention. But that's all changed now. And my voice is not as good as it used to be.

Lara: Of course it is! It's improved, in my opinion. Isn't it funny! I hated being in plays when I was a child, I'd do anything to avoid acting, and look at me now, I'm a full-time drama teacher.

Jack: Yes, I often wonder why you didn't become an actor rather than a teacher. You seemed to have all the qualities …

Lara: Yes, it makes me sad to think about it. I'd be earning lots of money now! Anyway, about that part in my play. How about this? I'll send you a copy of the play and you can have a look at it and then you can decide …

Jack: I'll do that, but I can't promise I'll say yes, OK? Now, listen, why don't you have the play a week later? That would give you time to find an actor and …

Lara: Oh, that would disappoint everyone, I can't do that. We'll talk again after the weekend. I must go now. Do give me a call. Bye!

Jack: Bye! I'll call you on Monday.

TEST TWO   PART ONE

Example:
Which musical instrument will the man buy?

Man: My daughter will be 12 next Saturday, and I've promised her a musical instrument. She thinks she's going to get a piano!

Woman: Oh dear. That's expensive, and then she might not play it very often. Why not get her a guitar, or a trumpet? There's always time to get her a piano when she's a bit older …

Man: No, I'll get her what she wants. I don't think she'd like a trumpet. And she's already got a guitar. She's quite good at it.

1 At what time will the art gallery open this weekend?

Man: If you're planning a visit to the Modern Art Gallery this coming weekend, take note of a change in opening hours. The gallery will open at a quarter past eleven, that's an hour later than usual because of repairs to the main hall. The closing time is unchanged, 6 p.m. From next week, opening hours go back to normal, that is we open from 9.30 a.m. to 5 p.m. Monday to Friday – and we're open 10.15 to 6 p.m. at weekends.

2 What will the woman order for lunch?

Man: I come to this restaurant every day for lunch and the food's always good. I don't know about you, but I'm very hungry. I'll have a large pizza and a salad.

Woman: The salad sounds great, I'll have some too. But I never eat a lot for lunch, so a pizza's too much, really. A bowl of soup and a roll. That'll be enough for me.

Man: You can then try their delicious ice-cream. It's really good.

Woman: Maybe next time. I only want a light meal today.

3 Where did the man find the handbag?

Woman: Thank you so much for returning my handbag, I realized I'd left it at the restaurant as soon as I got home. I'll never put it under my chair again, it's a very bad habit!

Man: It's not a good idea, no. Maybe you should hang it from the back of your chair, then you'd see it as you leave.

Woman: That's not very safe. Best place is on a chair near me really – where I can keep an eye on it.

Man: Yes. And check that you've got everything before leaving.

4 How did the man get to his office yesterday?

Man: I hope the bus will run on time today. Yesterday I got on it at 8.15 and there was so much traffic in the centre, it was 9 o'clock by the time I got to the office.

Woman: Why didn't you get off and walk?

Man: That's what I usually do, walk. It only takes 20 minutes on foot, but I was carrying a heavy briefcase full of documents.

Woman: Then what you needed was a taxi. It was silly not to take one.

5 What piece of furniture do they decide to buy first?

Woman: I saw a chest of drawers which would go really well in our bedroom. Only £150, in beautiful dark wood.

Man: But we need a new table for the dining room, don't we? And a new sofa. I thought they were far more urgent.

Woman: Well, we've got an old table – so that can wait. You're right about the sofa, though. It must come first. Pity, though. The chest of drawers seems such good value.

Man: Well, let's get what we need most and see how much money we have after that.

6 What will they do on Saturday afternoon?

Woman 1: After my tennis lesson on Saturday morning, do you want to meet me for lunch? We could then go to the cinema. There are a couple of very good films on.

Woman 2: It's OK for you. You'll have a lot of exercise in the morning, but I won't. I think I'd prefer to do something more active, like swimming or …

Woman 1: Well, the swimming pool's open in the evening. We could have a swim then, after the cinema.

Woman 2: OK. But I think I'll follow your example and start taking tennis lessons soon.

7 What's the weather like at the seaside today?

Woman: Weather conditions in the hills today are perfect for walking – temperatures about 20 degrees and sunny most of the time with a bit of cloud at midday. By the sea it's a different story. The wind has brought a large amount of cloud to this area and it's likely that we won't see the sun here for the rest of the day. Temperatures will be pleasant, though, probably not below 18 degrees.

TEST TWO   PART TWO

Host: My guest today is a chef called Patrick Simmons. Patrick, how did you decide to become a chef?

Patrick: I'd always loved to cook. My mother encouraged me to go to a Cooking School – just to learn new dishes. Neither of us were thinking of cooking as a career then. While I was at the School, one of my teachers asked me if I'd like to be a weekend chef at a local hotel. It was good for the practical side of my course, so I took the job. I didn't really need it – my mother was paying for everything.

Host: Was it a good job?

Patrick: Oh yes. I only worked from 5 till 10 p.m., which was great, and I learnt a lot. But after a year or so, it became a bit boring. You see, the hotel was well-known for its weekend menus, which were always kept more or less the same – not a real challenge for me. So, I gave it up and moved to a job in a restaurant. The hotel manager wasn't at all pleased with my decision!

Host: Did you enjoy being a restaurant chef?

Patrick: Well, this was an Italian restaurant and I was able to look into a different aspect of the job. My menus were special, like in no other Italian restaurant, but the owner said I had to find cheaper ingredients. And I managed to do that – while keeping the same quality. He made me realize that the business side of the restaurant industry is just as important as the creative one.

Host: Of all your recipes, which ones are you really proud of?

Patrick: My chicken dishes are good, but not as good as a friend of mine's, a French chef. Now, my bread recipes – that's something I'm really proud of. I think I've produced some of the best. Many people think breadmaking's the easiest thing, but it isn't. Now I'm creating new vegetable recipes, but it takes time to develop recipes and I'm not happy with them yet.

Host: What's the most important skill a chef needs?

Patrick: All chefs are great cooks, but that alone doesn't make you a good chef ... Nothing's more important for a chef than the ability to pay attention to what cooks and customers are saying, to know in which direction to take the food. This is a skill many chefs lack. Other things are less important, like keeping up-to-date with the latest technical developments – I think we all do that.

Host: What advice would you give those who are studying to become chefs?

Patrick: I'd say, it's OK to work hard at getting your qualifications, but you should give yourself time for other things. Many teachers at Cooking School have been chefs for years. Get to know them and interview them about how they got started as chefs. For example, was it a full-time or part-time job? That sort of knowledge will make it easier to find the right job once you leave Cooking school.

Host: Patrick, many thanks for talking to us.

TEST TWO   PART THREE

Woman: Hello, everybody. I hope you're enjoying your stay in this great city. Tomorrow we're off to the countryside, as you know, and I want to go through the programme with you. We'll have to start early to make the most of our day out, so breakfast will be served at 8.30. You'll have about half an hour for that, and then I'll come and see you all in the dining room. Please be there at 9 o'clock. We'll then walk together to our bus, which will be parked outside the hotel, and we'll be off at 9.15.

We'll be on the bus for about three hours, but we'll have several short breaks and I promise you, you won't be bored! There are wonderful views along the way, of beautiful lakes and rivers. Then at 12.30, we'll stop for an hour in the forest, to have a picnic lunch. We'll then drive on a bit longer and arrive at our final destination – the hills.

Now, the afternoon programme. I know many of you are very fit and looking forward to a good hill walk. But that's not everyone's idea of a good day out! So, there'll be other activities as well. You may want to have a look at a village, which isn't far, and is very interesting, or you may want to go and see how a local farm works. And if you're a good swimmer, you may prefer to dive into the lake or take a boat trip.

Now, what to bring with you. It'll be colder in the hills than here, so a warm jacket is essential. You'll be in the sun for a long time, so don't forget a hat. It's important. And don't worry about food – we'll provide sandwiches, drinks and even biscuits and sweets. Right, any questions?

TEST TWO   PART FOUR

Diana: Hi, James. I've got some photos of my trip to Africa to show you. Have you got a minute?

James: Oh, yes. Let's have a look. Great, a family of elephants! How did you manage to get so near them? I always take my wildlife photos from a safe distance.

Diana: It can be dangerous if the elephants get frightened, for example. But I was there with a guide, and he said it was OK … I'm not such a good photographer, really. I've just got a great camera!

James: Why do people say that a good camera is all you need? It's so untrue! I own a really expensive camera and I know my photos aren't nearly as good as these … Anyway, you must be really pleased with these photos.

Diana: I am. I'm even thinking of doing a photography course at college. I think I can make a living taking photos for wildlife magazines. And I'd get to travel. I told my parents the other day, thinking they'd disapprove, but they were very encouraging.

James: Well, I'd also like to take a course in photography, but just a short one, to learn to take really good photos underwater. I went scuba diving last summer and took just a few photos of some lovely tropical fish. It was so much simpler than I'd imagined!

Diana: I tried underwater photography once and the results were so disappointing! You know what? I've got a list of all the courses available at college. I'll have a look and I'll call you if there's anything on underwater photography.

James: Thank you! By the way, I heard they're looking for somebody to take photos at the school end-of-year party. Would you be able to do it?

Diana: I don't like taking photos of people, it's so boring.

James: They really do need somebody to do it.

Diana: Tell them I'll do it this time, but they shouldn't expect me to do it every year!

TEST THREE   PART ONE

Example:
Which musical instrument will the man buy?

Man: My daughter will be 12 next Saturday, and I've promised her a musical instrument. She thinks she's going to get a piano!

Woman: Oh dear. That's expensive, and then she might not play it very often. Why not get her a guitar, or a trumpet? There's always time to get her a piano when she's a bit older …

Man: No, I'll get her what she wants. I don't think she'd like a trumpet. And she's already got a guitar. She's quite good at it.

1   What present do they decide to give their uncle?

Woman: It's Uncle Bob's birthday on Saturday. I was thinking, maybe we could buy him a nice tie …

Man: You must be joking. A tie's so personal. Let's get him the usual thing, a couple of CDs. He likes adding to his collection of classical music.

Woman: Oh, come on, can't we be a bit more original this time? How about a lamp for his desk? They're not expensive …

Man: That's not a bad idea. Better than a tie, no doubt! Can you buy it, please? I've got so much work …

2   What does Margaret look like now?

Woman: I saw Margaret in the street the other day and I hardly recognized her. I hadn't seen her for ages, of course. She no longer wears glasses, which makes her look so different.

Man: Yes, and her hair's now blonde rather than brown …

Woman: That's right. And she used to wear it quite short, didn't she?

Man: When she was at college she did, but she's had it long for at least three years. Anyway, she's still the same lovely person, isn't she?

3   Where will they have the party?

Man 1: We'll need to think again about our party. I said we could have it in my house, but if we're inviting 20 people, then my sitting room's not large enough. Maybe we could have it in a restaurant instead, or in the park, by the lake.

Man 2: I see what you mean. But that would make it a very different kind of party, wouldn't it? The easiest thing, I think, is to invite fewer people and carry on as we'd planned.

Man 1: OK, let's have a look at our list, then …

4   Which magazine does the woman read regularly?

Man: Can I borrow your *Computer World* magazine?

Woman: Yes, you can keep it. I've finished with it. It's the one magazine I read as soon as it comes on Tuesdays. I get *Fashion Today* as well, but I read it if and when I have the time, which means I often throw it away unread! You buy *Health and Fitness*, don't you? Is it any good?

Man: It's excellent. You can have it after I've read it.

Woman: Thank you, but I think I'll start buying it myself. I must get fit for the summer!

5   Which music event is free?

Man: Book now for the series of spring concerts at the Lloyd Theatre. Our varied programme will start with an opera evening on the 17th. As usual there's no charge for this first event but tickets are limited, so you must book now if you don't want to be disappointed. On the 18th there's a concert by the Youth Orchestra and on the 20th an evening with The Dolphins, the rock group from Liverpool. Ticket prices for both performances are £25 and you can book by telephone or online.

6   At what time will Brenda phone Jackie tomorrow?

Brenda: Hi, Jackie, it's Brenda. I'd very much like your opinion about something. Can you talk now?

Jackie: Sorry, Brenda. I'm on my way out. It's a quarter past ten now and I have a meeting in 15 minutes. Could you call me tomorrow at a quarter past eight, please, if that isn't too early for you …

Brenda: Oh, that's fine. I'm usually up by half past seven!

Jackie: OK then. I'll be expecting your call. Bye for now!

7   What was the boy doing when the lights went off?

Boy: When the lights went off, I decided to go to bed, although it was only 9 o'clock. An hour earlier, I'd phoned Mario about a school project we're doing together. We had a long chat – about our homework and about football. He told me about the Liverpool versus Manchester United match on the telly. Then I felt hungry and I started making myself some supper, thinking I'd have it in front of the telly – I was really looking forward to that. That's when it all went dark.

TEST THREE   PART TWO

Man: And now for some reviews of what's on TV this weekend … Now, Saturday first …

At 5.30 on BBC 2, you can see *Wildlife of Madagascar*. We see, not the most popular region in this great island, but one of the least visited areas, the amazing mountains of the north-east. Great scenery, but Madagascar has some of the most incredible animals. We hear about them – the indri, for example, which looks a bit like a monkey and is almost completely black. But we hardly ever get to see any of them, which is a pity.

Same time on Channel 4, *The Witness*, the best drama series on TV for ages, comes to an end. This six-part series about lawyer Peter Barnes has kept our interest alive for weeks, and I can only tell you that you should prepare yourselves for a very unexpected conclusion. As usual, though, excellent performances from Jack Lloyds as the bright lawyer and Paul Winters as his quiet secretary.

At 7 o'clock, there's *The Bill Smith Show* on BBC 4, with a comic performer who is good, but who was funnier when he first started, five years ago. If you remember his show as it was then, you'll notice the difference. The laughs are still there, but some of his sketches often seem too long. Good entertainment for all the family, though, if that's what you want.

Now, Sunday. There's been a change on BBC 2 – *Men of Iron* will be at 8.30 instead of 10.30. Make a note of that because this is about Brunel, the man who built the greatest railway in England in the 19th century and also wanted to create a high-speed transport link between New York and London. It's one of the best history programmes for a long, long time.

At 6 on Channel 4 there's *Secret Job*, the detective series based on a best-selling novel. In this episode, we watch Detective Joe Barker using his skills to solve a murder mystery. Although it is similar to lots of other detective stories, the quality of the acting makes it special and really worth watching.

Finally, on BBC 1 at 9.30, *Student Life* is a new series about a group of university students and their busy lives in the big city of London. In this first part, we meet Louise and Clara, two biology students who share a small flat. I don't think there's enough in this series to keep young audiences interested, unless there is a marked improvement next week.

That's all for today. Enjoy …

TEST THREE   PART THREE

John: Hello. I'm John Grey and I'm here to tell you about some very interesting leisure courses at Lancaster college. Two of them are three months long, the other two go on for six months, but they'll all start at 6 p.m. and continue until 9 on Mondays. I know some of you would prefer Fridays, but we've got other activities then.

All the courses will be in the College building – which, if you don't know, is facing the post office, next to the museum. These courses are not just about art, you'll learn the first steps to becoming artists!

Now, first something about the three-month courses. Both of them begin on the 18th February, followed by a simple test on the 22nd May. 'Play an instrument' is a course where you are given a choice between learning to play the piano or the violin. I'm sorry to say we are not able to offer the guitar as a choice this time, but we hope to be able to offer it next year. The other 3-month course is called 'Painting for Beginners', which will teach you the basic skills, including how to draw.

Now, the six-month courses will start in April and finish in September, but I won't have the actual dates till next week. One of them is a 'Modern Dance' course which I'm sure will be very popular, and the other is called 'What makes a good Photograph?', and you'll need to bring your own camera for this course.

Finally, prices. The 3-month courses cost 60 euros and it's 150 euros for six months, with discounts for students. You'll have to pay for the course books separately but the price of the course includes the certificate that you get at the end and use of the library and computer rooms.

OK, if you need more information …

TEST THREE   PART FOUR

Nora: Sam, I'm thinking of applying for a summer job, a job in an office – you know – writing letters, answering the phone, that sort of thing.

Sam: It doesn't sound very exciting.

Nora: I know. That's why I want a job like that. I already have enough excitement in my life! Now, you had a job in a lawyers' office last year. How was it?

Sam: Oh, OK. It was a simple job – typing out documents and reports and welcoming clients – but I learnt about organizing meetings and things like that. It certainly wasn't a waste of time.

Nora: You didn't have to sit in front of a boring computer all day.

Sam: No, I had a lot of variety. I don't understand why you'd find computer work boring though. I'd quite like a job where I have to do nothing except computer work.

Nora: Are you also looking for a summer job?

Sam: I've already got one, in a Travel Shop office. It was advertised on the school notice board. I hope I'll be able to use the German I learnt at school. I don't speak it as well as you do, but I think I'll manage.

Nora: Oh, but your German's excellent. Is the money good?

Sam: It's less than I got in last year's job, but it should be interesting, so I don't mind.

Nora: Hmm … In my case, the only reason for wanting to work in the summer is that I need the money, so that's what I'll look at first of all.

Sam: Probably the best place to look is in the local paper. And the Internet, of course. I could look at some Internet websites and let you know if I see anything that seems like what you want.

Nora: That's very kind of you but I'm sure I'll manage to find something by the end of this week at the latest.

Sam: OK, let me know how it goes.

TEST FOUR   PART ONE

Example:
Which musical instrument will the man buy?

Man: My daughter will be 12 next Saturday, and I've promised her a musical instrument. She thinks she's going to get a piano!

Woman: Oh dear. That's expensive, and then she might not play it very often. Why not get her a guitar, or a trumpet? There's always time to get her a piano when she's a bit older …

Man: No, I'll get her what she wants. I don't think she'd like a trumpet. And she's already got a guitar. She's quite good at it.

1   What did the man dislike about the party?

Woman: How was Sally's party?

Man: Great fun. She'd organized lots of party games, made me realize I'm not too old for that sort of thing. I can't say the same about the music … You see, there wasn't a single piece I liked!

Woman: Oh, dear. What about the food?

Man: It was just sandwiches – but nobody was expecting a big meal. And there was a birthday cake of course.

2   For which concert should you book tickets in advance?

Woman: Now, if you have no plans for the weekend and you're a music lover, there's lots to do. On Saturday there's the Spanish Guitars group at the City Hall. On Saturday as well, a piano concert by Carol Finlay at the Apollo theatre. This is a small theatre so book your tickets soon if you don't want to be disappointed. On Sunday there's a violin concert by the popular Orange Strings Group, at the Market theatre, with tickets available only on the day.

3   What will they buy for their friend Jill?

Girl 1: Now, about Jill's birthday. I don't think we should give her a T-shirt again. I saw a great sun hat we could buy her. She's going on holiday to the seaside soon.

Girl 2: I agree about not giving her a T-shirt! But she was wearing a sun hat the other day, remember? Why don't we get her a beach bag? It wouldn't cost more than a sun hat.

Girl 1: And it's probably more original. Let's do that.

4   What will the weather be like in the hills tomorrow?

Woman: And now the weather forecast for the next two days in the hills. We'll see the last of the rain tonight but it'll remain cloudy and cold for the next twenty-four hours. By the end of the day tomorrow, temperatures may be as low as zero degrees. There'll be sunshine at last the day after tomorrow, with temperatures slowly rising, and there will be a light wind from the east. And that was your forecast.

5   Where is the present now?

Woman: So where's the present for Maria? We didn't leave it at home, did we?

Man: Well, I thought you had it in your bag. I saw you picking it up from the dining room table.

Woman: Let me see … I did pick it up … Oh, I know what happened. I put it back down on there again to answer the phone. We'll have to go back and get it.

6   Which job will the girl apply for?

Boy: So, have you decided which job you'll apply for?

Girl: Yes, I spent all yesterday thinking about it. The job in the shoe shop is well paid, it's a nice place to work, ten minutes by bus. At the bookshop I get a bit less money, but it's a ten-minute walk so I can save money on transport and save time. So I'm going for it. The job in the furniture shop seemed really interesting, but they open on Saturday afternoon, which I'm definitely not keen on.

7   At what time is the *World Music* radio programme today?

Man: And now some information about changes to this afternoon's radio programmes. From midday, we shall bring you reports on the Grand Tennis Championships live from the Sports Club. Therefore, there will be no afternoon play at 1.15 and the 2.15 *World Music* programme will start at the later time of 3.15, after the news. There will be no changes to our evening programmes.

TEST FOUR   PART TWO

Host: Hello. In the studio today is Philip Samson, the mountain bike racer. Philip, how did you start riding mountain bikes?

Philip: Well, I only discovered mountain bikes when I was 16. I was keen on lots of other sports, but mountain biking – I believed – was not something I'd be good at. Then there was a bicycle race in my village and I just wanted to take part – knowing I'd probably be last.

Host: Your family must be proud of you.

Philip: Well, my mother is. Before I left home to ride in my first World Cup five years ago, I said to her that I felt I'd win, because I'd trained so much. She replied I'd be lucky to come third or fourth! She wanted me to win of course, but she didn't really believe I could do it back then. Now she's always at the finishing line among all my fans!

Host: How do you feel after winning an important race?

Philip: Oh, wonderful. Sometimes the television's there, wanting to interview me, but I go straight to where all my fans are – they want autographs – so I sign my name hundreds of times. I'm always happy to do it, though I refuse to have conversations with them at this point … They know they can see me later for that, when I've had a rest.

Host: What makes you better than other racers?

Philip: Oh, at the highest level we all work hard and make sure we have the best possible bikes. I do a lot of cross-country racing, over hills and on difficult roads, as every other racer does. But on top of that I do a lot of really hard gym work – and I think this is it – other riders spend most of their time riding their bikes and less on other training.

Host: Do you read mountain bike magazines?

Philip: Although there are so many mountain bike riders now, few of them actually buy magazines, so the publishers are always worrying about sales … I read a few of them, but if you look at them carefully, you'll find reports and interviews about leisure riding, plenty of that, but hardly anything on actual races. That means professional racers would find little of interest in them.

Host: Finally, you're now 32. Will you continue to race for many years?

Philip: Yes, but I have other plans as well. A few months ago I had an offer to do TV advertisements for mountain bikes. I wasn't sure about it then, but now I need the income – and I think it'll be good for the sport – getting more people interested. I've also had an offer to appear in a film – a thriller, but it would take too much of my time. I also refused an offer to write a book about my career, for the same reason.

Host: Philip, thank you for talking to us.

TEST FOUR   PART THREE

Peter: Hello. My name is Peter Don and I'm here to tell you about a great holiday on the west coast of Sri Lanka. Sri Lanka is a lovely island in the Indian ocean. Many visitors stay on the west coast because it's got everything they need – sandy beaches which are among the most beautiful in the world, wonderful nature walks and an incredible bird life.

The hotel we have chosen for you is in a very peaceful location. Behind the hotel, there are large tropical gardens with an amazing variety of trees – well over seventy of them – and about ninety types of bird. All the hotel rooms are light and airy, with both air conditioning and a ceiling fan for your comfort – and attractive furniture made locally.

The holiday we offer you includes several visits to interesting places, and I'll give you two examples now. As you know, tea is very important to Sri Lanka's economy, so we'll take you to a plantation, where tea is grown, to taste different teas and learn to tell the difference between high and low quality tea. And have you ever wondered what goes into teabags? Well, you'll have the opportunity to find out how they make them!

We have also planned a visit to a Sri Lanka country house where you'll be able to talk to the owner and admire her collection of paintings by local artists, as well as enjoy a typical meal served in great style.

A 12-night stay in Sri Lanka costs between 250 and 350 pounds, depending on the time of year. The price always includes the accommodation and the tours but if you want me to arrange your flights or your travel insurance, you have to pay for that separately.

If you'd like a leaflet with more details, please call me on …

TEST FOUR   PART FOUR

David: Any plans for Saturday, Carol? I'm going for a walk in the hills with a few friends. If you want to come …

Carol: Well, thank you, but I'm going to my aunt's for the day. She's really nice and I always have a good time with my cousins, so I think it'll be a great day.

David: Of course. Well, I can't wait for Saturday and Sunday! I had to spend last weekend writing a report – my boss wanted it on his desk on Monday morning! I'm glad I don't have to do any more this weekend …

Carol: Umm … working at weekends is no fun, is it? I've got a bit of work to do, but it should only take an hour … So what are you doing after your walk?

David: Well, the Novo Band are here – did you know? They're playing at the Apollo Theatre.

Carol: Yeah, but it's very difficult to get tickets, isn't it? Have you got yours?

David: Not yet. Now I think of it, it may be too late. Oh, well …

Carol: Why don't you go to the cinema instead? There's a great thriller on at the Odeon – *Mystery at Sea*. I saw it last week.

David: I heard about it, yes. The cinema's not my idea of fun, really. Sooner or later you can see most good films on TV.

Carol: Yeah, that's true. So, anything for Sunday?

David: I think I'll play tennis. What about you?

Carol: I'd like to go surfing. I'm not like you, I usually avoid sport at weekends – I think I'm a bit lazy! But I tried surfing, when I was on holiday last year – and I really enjoyed it …

David: If you want, I could come surfing with you. I can play tennis another time.

Carol: Oh, no, I'm only a beginner. You'd be bored.

David: I'm not that good myself! I need a lot of practice!

Carol: Really? OK then!

TEST ONE

PART ONE
1 Instructions
2 Question 1
3 Question 2
4 Question 3
5 Question 4
6 Question 5
7 Question 6
8 Question 7

PART TWO
9 Questions 8–13

PART THREE
10 Questions 14–19

PART FOUR
11 Questions 20–25

TEST TWO

PART ONE
12 Instructions
13 Question 1
14 Question 2
15 Question 3
16 Question 4
17 Question 5
18 Question 6
19 Question 7

PART TWO
20 Questions 8–13

PART THREE
21 Questions 14–19

PART FOUR
22 Questions 20–25

TEST THREE

PART ONE
23 Instructions
24 Question 1
25 Question 2
26 Question 3
27 Question 4
28 Question 5
29 Question 6
30 Question 7

PART TWO
31 Questions 8–13

PART THREE
32 Questions 14–19

PART FOUR
33 Questions 20–25

TEST FOUR

PART ONE
34 Instructions
35 Question 1
36 Question 2
37 Question 3
38 Question 4
39 Question 5
40 Question 6
41 Question 7

PART TWO
42 Questions 8–13

PART THREE
43 Questions 14–19

PART FOUR
44 Questions 20–25